INTERCEPT AND BOARD

SITIONS

OF 0800Z

LY 1972

COOK IN
Anchor
Pt.
C Cleare

KENAI PEN

Augustine I.

Kamishak
Bay

Cape Douglas

C. Elizabeth

Barren Is

Portlock Bank

Katmai
Vol

Shuyak I

SHELIKOF STRAIT

Kodiak I. ★ CITRUS

C. Chiniak

KODIAK

C. Ikolik

Dangerous
Cape

Albatross Bank

Trinity Is

Chirikof I

Giacomini Seamo

★ CLOVER

★ WACHUSETT

1 2 3 4 JAPANESE
★ ★ ★ ★ F/V

Patton Seamount

Gilbert Seamount

Parker Seamount

RTON
LAND

★

ALL POSITIONS ARE AS OF 0800Z 13 JULY 1972

INTERCEPT
AND
BOARD

By

Emery Huntoon

Binford & Mort

Thomas Binford, Publisher

2536 S.E. Eleventh • Portland, Oregon 97202

TO THE MEN OF THE U.S. COAST GUARD
AND TO MY LATE BROTHER CLYDE,
WHO LOVED THE SEA,
I DEDICATE THIS BOOK.

PREFACE

The opportunity to prepare a study of just one of the many incidents of seizures and detainment of foreign fishing vessels involving the U.S. Coast Guard offered a welcome challenge. While reading material pertinent to fishing limits, illegal gear and unethical methods has been growing rapidly during the past year, and while many of the incidents have been treated as endangering United States foreign relations, more public exposure has been considered necessary.

I have attempted to bring into focus the varied and important effects of the impact of this incident on the future of the American fishing industry. The task was difficult because of the many governmental bureaus and offices involved, as well as the scattering of the personnel who were directly involved. Data which would be useful in clarifying specific actions was frequently found to be classified, and some questions completely and deliberately ignored.

This study was made over a two-year period prior to June, 1975. I have traveled extensively through different parts of the United States to examine library and newspaper materials available, and to consult with Coast Guard, fisheries, government, and food-processing personnel, as well as commercial fishermen, about those relevant matters with which they were most familiar.

The printed records were carefully examined. Numerous official and unofficial releases were given attention. Hundreds of pamphlets, reports, and newspaper accounts were part of the mass of material accumulated and considered. No pains were spared in obtaining the information which was deemed appropriate.

E.H.

CONTENTS

1. "Stand By" 1
2. "Change Course" 8
3. The Chase 13
4. Setting the Trap 23
5. "Full Speed Ahead" 29
6. "Prepare for Boarding" 36
7. News Censored 41
8. The Gap Closes 48
9. Briefing 55
10. Taking Over 64
11. Resistance? 69
12. Securing the Vessel 75
13. Another Try 81
14. No Help 88
15. New Quarters 94
16. An Escape? 100
17. Camping Out 107
18. Boarding Party Split 114
19. Steering Problem 121
20. Net Retrieving 128
21. Rendezvous 140
22. "Convoy" 147
23. No Greeting 155
24. The Evidence 164
25. Shore Leave 171
26. The Secret 176
27. Interrogation 183
28. The Whaler Lands 189
29. End of a Fine Ship 192
    Epilogue 195

ACKNOWLEDGMENTS

It is not possible to acknowledge all those individuals who rendered some assistance on this project, nor do many of them desire me to do so. However, three of those most helpful were: Commander Bruno Forsterer, Lt. Commander Robert Stracener, and Fire Controlman First Class Fred Glass, all of the U.S. Coast Guard.

For the kindness and assistance given me so generously in collecting background material I also want to thank: Wendell Wyatt, Portland attorney, Congressman from Oregon First District from 1964 to 1974; Oregon Congressman Robert Duncan; Nevin May, past president, Ketchikan Trollers Association; National Marine Fisheries Service Staff; and Theodore T. Bugas, executive secretary, Columbia River Salmon and Tuna Packers Association.

For the drawings so well done and generously donated, I thank my friend, John Cox. For the excellent photographs, I thank Lt. Commander Robert Stracener, the U.S. Coast Guard, and the National Marine Fisheries Service. For the interest, tolerance and patience shown me, I thank my wife.

E.H.

INTRODUCTION

Emery Huntoon's tale of the last Alaska patrol of the U.S.C.G.C. *Wachusett* is an excellent chronicle of both the day-to-day routine aboard a cruising, high-endurance Coast Guard cutter and of that always-anticipated moment of high action—boarding and seizure.

The author's very thorough research will give the reader not only a realistic picture of an operational mission but also an inner glimpse into the lives and attitudes of the men performing the mission. Emery Huntoon has also turned in a fine piece of reporting on the current state of the international fisheries and their impact on our ocean resources.

In defense of a superior group of officers and men, I will take exception to some of Emery's personality portrayals though I agree that individuals of a similar nature can and do serve aboard our ships. Even though *Intercept and Board* is fictional in part, the reader will join me in reliving an exciting account of a high-seas incident that actually occurred.

B.A. Forsterer,
CDR, USCG (ret.)

1. "STAND BY"

The sky was gray, as was the water, with low clouds spitting a fine mist as the U.S. Coast Guard Cutter *Wachusett* sliced through the waters of the Pacific, off the coast of Alaska, on her way to Anchorage that late afternoon in July, 1972.

For those who could see her she made an unforgettable picture with her clean, white exterior cutting completely through an occasional wave. Each dip would bring portions of salt water rinsing the sparkling superstructure and making the red, white and blue Coast Guard insignia together with her black-lettered "44" that much more impressive.

While the cutter made an awe-inspiring picture from the outside, she could make a similar impression from the inside. She was clean and well cared for by both officers and enlisted men even though a large percent of her gear was of World War II vintage.

The eight-to-ten-foot waves she was cutting through now were nothing new to her. She had handled heavier seas on many occasions. All she needed was someone at the helm who could read her little intricacies. She hadn't been equipped with an automatic pilot, forcing whoever was at her wheel to wrestle the wheel first one way and then the other in order to maintain anything resembling a straight course.

The lookouts who would normally be standing on the starboard and port wings were absent on this occasion and for good reason. When the "44" would disappear into a wave, the near freezing water would have surely soaked anyone standing outside, if not washing them overboard. The radar screen was absent of pips, indicating there shouldn't be any obstruction within miles of them and allowing the lookouts to perform their duties inside the pilothouse.

They would be required to take turns relieving the helmsman, so why put the men through the task of changing to foul weather gear every hour if it wasn't a necessity?

When the spray settled between waves, the noise of the windshield wipers slapped continuously, enabling them to see a reasonable distance. The monotony made this a boring task before the end of a four-hour watch. Both lookouts and helmsman were happy to see their relief come.

Normally there was not a great deal of conversation when it was time for the change of watch, but this was a little different. The entire crew was aware of the fact that liberty was to be theirs when they reached Anchorage, and that couldn't come too soon.

"Another of those days," said Seaman Carter, as he took over the wheel and acknowledged the course to be taken.

"Yep, and as usual the 'Old Girl' has a mind of her own. She doesn't seem to be very eager to get to Anchorage," replied the retiring helmsman. Before leaving he pointed to the thermometer saying, "There it is the high for the day again, just reached 45 degrees. I guess that one day we had this month when it reached 65 is the only one we are going to have on this cruise."

Seaman Kelly would have stayed a bit longer and chatted with Carter, the two seeming to have quite a bit in common. Neither had been in the Coast Guard long, and it was the first cruise of any great length for them. A frown from Ensign Jefferson, serving as officer of the deck, discouraged him from staying on even though he was in a talkative mood. He reluctantly headed for the mess deck where he knew there would be a cup of coffee and plenty of crew members to talk to.

"Boy, I don't think I could take this kind of duty for any real length of time, being confined as we are," Kelly was saying to himself as he entered the mess hall and picked up a cup of coffee. As he walked over and sat across from Petty Officer First Class Fred Glass he remarked, "Damn, you are about the only one on board who can put up with this."

"What the hell are you talking about?" Glass responded, looking at the young man as though he had flipped his cork.

"I mean this confinement. Geez, I'm getting claustrophobia, and it's only been a few weeks. You spent eight years in the submarine service so maybe you're used to it, but I'm sure as hell not, and doubt if I ever will be."

"Relax, kid. You'll get the swing of it in time," Glass said trying to reassure him, then adding, "You just have to remember that the 'Old Girl' is only 255 feet long, with a beam of 43 feet, and with 130 enlisted men and 14 officers on board that just isn't a hell of a lot of elbow room. So if you keep your elbows close to your body you won't have any trouble."

"What do you expect to do, go sun-bathing every day?" the assistant cook said, acknowledging that he had been eavesdropping on their conversation. Then before Kelly could answer he added, "Say, Glass, how you guys coming on the repair work after our little fire in Dutch Harbor?"

"Not very well," Glass answered, and then because he didn't really want to talk about the matter with the assistant cook, he turned back to Kelly. He had never been able to cultivate a real liking for Timmons, the assistant cook. The fellow just seemed to have a knack for rubbing people the wrong way. He was a short, squatty fellow, with beady eyes that just seemed to provoke others when he looked at them.

Glass was hoping Timmons would get the hint and leave, when he turned back to Kelly and said, "Just remember, kid, we have a liberty coming up in a few hours in Anchorage, and then you can get yourself a little girl friend, and then everything will be fine for a few weeks."

"You know I don't mess around with girls. I have a girl friend back in Seattle and that is enough for me," Kelly came back a little irritated with Glass. He had always admired Glass and he thought that the feeling was mutual, but now he wondered why Glass was putting the needle into him like that with Timmons still standing there taking it all in.

Glass could see the hurt look on his face, but went on with, "Well there are plenty of saloons, movie houses, and I'll bet there is even a library there, if you don't think ours here on the ship is complete enough. After all what else could a guy ask?"

"Ah, to hell with you," was all Kelly could think of to say.

To ease the tension that he knew existed now, Glass said, "Don't forget when we get to Anchorage we will have a batch of mail to pick up, and there just could be a letter or two for you there."

And with that Kelly's eyes lit up and he was willing to talk some more, "All in all, this has been a pretty boring trip, wouldn't you say?"

Glass looked at him for a couple of minutes, remembering back when he had first gone into the service. He had been about the same age as Kelly was now, and had wondered from moment to moment what was going to happen next. He could well understand Kelly's desire to have some type of encouragement from someone who had spent years in the service. Glass could only guess that they had both been about the same height, five foot ten, at the time of enlistment, about the same weight—165 pounds—and probably about the only physical difference would have been the color of hair. Kelly had blond hair and didn't keep it cut as short as Glass always kept his dark brown hair, but after all, styles for young men had changed. His mind snapped back to the present while he debated with himself as to how he was going to answer Kell's question.

"Oh, I don't know as I would go so far as to call it a real boring trip," Glass answered. "After all, if you had been aboard on some of those trips where all we did was to sit in the middle of the Pacific, half way between San Francisco and Hawaii, and take a few samples out of the ocean and tell a few airplanes they were on course, you'd know what boredome really is."

"Well, at least you were able to get out on deck then. Right now the deck of this ship looks like a sluice box, except you'll never find a gold nugget," Kelly replied, taking another big swallow of his coffee and lighting up a cigarette.

"You'd better hang on to that cup," Glass said, as the cutter hit a wave solidly and cups slid across the mess table. The dishes rattled in the cupboards. "Must have been a pretty good-sized one there."

"Yea, there are a few waves like that," Kelly said, "I just came off the helm and some of those waves want to turn the ship completely around."

"Look at it this way, kid. You'll grow up with strong arms if you stay on the wheel of this ship," Glass commented. "That and the fact that we are making pretty good speed brings us that much closer to that liberty and those letters you're looking for."

Kelly ignored the last part of his friend's comment and said, "It's just a good thing I wasn't on the wheel when they had the competition down at San Diego last year. We would never have won that 'E' for ship control."

"Don't sweat it," Glass came back, "it's painted up there now. And in addition to ship control, we got operation readiness, engineering, and all-around good guys; I wouldn't be a bit surprised but that we can do it again."

Both looked up as Gunner's Mate "Moose" Kjiellin flopped his huge frame down beside Kelly. The crew had aptly nicknamed him "Moose." With his six feet three, and 280 pounds of bulk, there just was no other name that they could have hung on him. As he fingered his cup a little he turned to Glass and said, "How you coming with that repair, Glass?"

"You better just forget the fire control part of that gun out there," Glass answered. "You guys better figure you're on your own if there is any need for that gun."

"That bad, eh?"

"Yah, it's that bad," Glass answered. "You better hope there isn't any gunnery practice for the balance of this trip, or they'll find out what a lousy shot you are."

"Bull s---. We never did really need you fire control clowns anyway. We only let you in on the action because you'd have a hell of a time finding work someplace else," Moose shot back. Then because he didn't really want to start any fuss with anyone he added, "The only thing this ship needs is a good set of pumps. That seems to be about all we do is run around finding distressed fishing boats and either keep them afloat with our pumps or tow 'em into some port. Outside of gunnery practice that gun out there hasn't had any real use since we were over in Vietnam."

In an effort to change the subject again, Glass turned to Kelly and asked, "Say you just came off watch, did you hear any news about what time we are supposed to get into Anchorage?"

"Naw," Kelly replied. "They were talking about passing just south of Kodiak Island in a few hours, and if so that should put us in Anchorage sometime tomorrow afternoon, I'd say."

"Well, it can't be too soon for me," Moose piped up. "Hell, it's been a month since we left Seattle, hasn't it?"

"Just about," Glass replied. "I'm with you. I'll be glad when this cruise is over. But I suppose that will just be the beginning of our work getting that fire control system back in operation." Then realizing that he had opened the conversation about the fire control mechanism himself he added, "I've got to get back to 'Buck'; he's still up there working." Before anyone could say a word he was up and headed down the passageway toward the bow of the ship.

Conversation lagged for some time in the mess hall with most of the crew either concerning themselves with their coffee or magazines, until a messenger from the bridge burst into the hall looking for Radioman Joel Walton.

"You're wanted in the radio shack," he said and started to leave.

"Hey! What's up?" Moose asked of the messenger.

No one was really interested in having Moose as anything but a friend, so while someone else's question might have gone un-answered the messenger took just enough time to say, "Oh, there is a bunch of radio messages coming in right now, and 'Sparks' wants a little relief," and with that he was headed back toward the bridge.

"What the hell do you suppose that means?" someone piped up from the back of the hall.

"Well, I'd say they are busy notifying the mothers in Anchorage that Kelly here is going to be loose, and they had better get their young girls off the streets," Moose said, then adding, "You know it's us Coasties' job to save lives, regardless whether it's young girls or old fishermen." With that he let out a real belly laugh.

Kelly didn't think the remark had that much humor, and said as much. But as soon as he had shot back at Moose he realized he shouldn't have, and to avoid being caught in an argument he stormed out of the hall. He never had liked the way the big gunner's mate picked on him, but he also knew that he was no physical match for him.

"Why do you pick on the kid?" someone sitting near asked.

"It gives me something to do!" Moose came back, stroking his dark brown beard. Then not wanting to get all the fellows down on him, he changed the subject back to the radio messages with, "What do you suppose an overload of messages to us means?"

"More likely it's some fisherman that didn't get to cover in time. Maybe hit an iceberg and needs our pumps," David Thompson volunteered.

"Ah, why don't you go back to your test tubes?" Moose said. He never did have much respect for the Marine Science Tech. After all he had often thought—what is this Coast Guard coming to anyway? Bringing some young punk like him along to test the water. After all, salt water was salt water no matter where in this damned ocean you checked.

Thompson started to raise up from his bench as though to do battle, when the engines slowed. Because of the sudden slowing of the ship he was forced to grab the table for support, and by the time he had regained his balance the thought of challenging Moose had completely left his mind. Everyone in the hall looked at each other for an explanation of the ship's maneuver.

Before anyone could get a word out, the ship went into a heavy list as she was executing a turn.

"I guess whatever it is we are hot on it," Yeoman James said.

"It doesn't look like we will be getting our liberty clothes dirty for awhile anyway," piped one of the crew who had been drumming his fingers on the table top.

Another, who openly frowned because he had hoped to see a fight between Moose and Thompson, said sarcastically, "Oh, what the hell, we have to earn that raise the taxpayers granted us, don't we?"

"I'll tell you one thing," chimed in another, "they will pay hell getting me to re-enlist in this friggin' outfit, raise or no raise."

"Aw, come on, you never had it so good. If you got out to-morrow you'd find you would have to work for a living. Then what in hell would you do?" was shot back at him from some-where in the hall.

Someone else offered an answer with, "When he finds out what it is to work on the outside he'll be breaking down the door of the recruiting office, trying to get back in."

"Like hell I would."

"You don't think it was all that bad when you were in that bar back in Dutch Harbor," Moose said. "You were telling all the girls there how you were doing such a great job of saving the lives of the poor fishermen because they weren't able to take care of themselves."

With that everyone laughed, and things returned to normal. Someone moved over to the urn and said, "The coffee isn't half bad anyway."

2. "CHANGE COURSE"

Ever since the fire raced through the wiring of the fire control mechanism of the ship's five-inch gun at Dutch Harbor, Fred Glass had been busy. As First Class Fire Controlman it was his obligation to keep the fire power of the ship in the best possible working condition.

He and Third Class Fire Controlman Steve "Buck" Buckingham had spent hour after hour in the fire control shack on the flying bridge, trying at first to determine the extent of the damage, and later debating whether there was any hope of repair. After several days of chasing down the lines between the radar director and the gun, it became obvious that at least 12 new cables would have to be installed. The possibility of obtaining that type cable before they reached Seattle was just out of the question, and now after getting deeper into the problem they found that even the terminals on the director had been damaged in the fire, and possibly the entire director had been rendered useless. It was just a hopeless job to get that gun operating on anything but manual controls.

"It's pretty obvious we aren't going to get much out of what we have here, Buck," Glass said, as he stepped back to view the charred mess for the hundredth time since they had been working on it.

"I guess you are right about the cause," Steve replied. "It must have been that sudden surge of power that they threw on when we were docking. That sudden surge must have shorted through some of the cables, and from then on there wasn't much to keep it from arcing through the other cables."

"Regardless of the cause, we are going to have to rig up a way of firing that gun manually without setting off another fire, even though it's a damned sure thing that we won't be using it on this cruise," Fred commented, rubbing his chin at the same time, and hoping there was an easier way of doing it than there appeared to be.

If it hadn't been as serious as it was at the time, possibly they could have seen a little more humor in the original fire. They had been coming into the fueling dock at Dutch Harbor and had been closing the gap between the ship and the dock a little faster than usual, which was understandable. Considering the amount of tide and winds in the area at the time, a little extra speed could be useful for better control. Nevertheless the hard astern order had barely been executed and smoke started pouring out of the fire control shack. This smoke was a lot blacker and much more plentiful than that coming from the ship's stack located directly behind the shack. The dock crew, ready to secure the lines, were one scared bunch of boys. After all, the thought of a ship afire at their dock wasn't a happy one. Not only was there the ammunition aboard the ship to contend with, but there were thousands of gallons of fuel connected to the dock that would stand a good chance of going up in smoke.

The *Wachusett* had been fortunate in that all the dock crew did not run for hoses, but did take the ship's line and tie her up. Fred and some of the others who realized what the problem was started throwing switches that controlled the electricity feeding into the shack. Even though there was a separate power source available for a second run at the dock, no one felt it would be the smart thing to do. After all, there was much more fire fighting equipment ashore, if the fire proved to be serious.

An initial survey determined that the ship's electrical system had not suffered much damage. The bulk of the damage had been concentrated in the shack, the real heart of the ship's fire power. But, Hell, most crewmen thought, we haven't seriously fired that gun since the ship had its tour of duty in Vietnam waters, with the exception, of course, of gunnery practice. So why would anyone want to give serious concern to it?

That was fine for the rest of the crew to rationalize, but for Glass and Buckingham it meant work and lots of it. After all, weren't they responsible for the accurate firing of that piece? If they couldn't work out the problem enough to get the controls in working order they were at least going to have to figure a way to fire the piece manually without setting off a new fire.

The fire control pair had taped up as many places as they could find where the old cable insulation had burned through, but it was still problematical whether they had taken care of them all. Sure they could test each cable to see if it had been burned through but it still wouldn't tell them if the insulation had burned through in some unseen part of the line hidden between decks, and they didn't have enough equipment aboard to test all of the lines at the same time.

"Let's just pull those wires off the terminals and tape them up," Glass said. "It's a cinch that director is not going to do us any good for the balance of this trip."

"Boy, what a bunch of junk," Buckingham said, referring to the outdated gear in the shack.

"Well," Glass replied, "you have to keep in mind that this baby was built a few years ago. If I remember correctly her keel was laid in 1944, and she was commissioned in 1946, and that makes her about as old as you are! I doubt very much if they put more than $20 into her since she was built, with exception, of course, of those damned engines." He was thinking of the numerous times they had had trouble with them.

"You think we'll ever get that burned rubber smell out of here?" Buckingham asked, as he strained to get one of the terminal screws loosened up. Actually there shouldn't have been any problem; with his six-foot-two-inch stature and long-time athletic ability, the screws should have been easy pickings, except that they had been in place for a long time without being moved.

"Well, I'll tell you, Buck, if the weather ever clears up enough so we can leave one of the hatch doors open it would help. But to be perfectly honest, I'll just be glad when we get to Anchorage, so I can wash the taste out of my throat with a few drinks, and I don't mean water."

"Yeh, I have to admit that this job wouldn't be near as hard to look at after we've had a chance to have a few belts," Buckingham answered as he set a bottle of beer down that the two had smuggled up earlier in the day.

It wasn't common practice, but Glass, having access to the ship's beer supply—plus the fact that he had anticipated a hard day—had commandeered a couple bottles to quench their thirst.

With the exception of their work, the pair had little else in common. Buckingham, referred to mainly as "Buck," was 22 years old, and was about to complete his three-year hitch in service, planning to go to college as soon as he got out. Glass had served with the Navy close to eight years before leaving for a couple of years. He had worked as an electronics supervisor during the two years he was out, but deciding that type of living was not for him, he had returned to the service slightly more than a year before—this hitch, picking the Coast Guard rather than the Navy.

Another thing about which the two differed was the fact that "Buck" had recently got married, and had little or no responsibilities, while Glass had been married some ten years and was about to become a father for the second time. He already had a son "Mike," now eight years old. Glass himself was crowding 33 years of age.

Of course, none of these things altered their closeness when they had a job to do. While Glass had spent a good many years at the trade, "Buck" had always given the impression that he was interested in learning electronics, and as a result they got on famously.

"Jeeze, that was a tough one," Buck said as he finally broke the terminal screw loose that he had been working so desperately on. He glanced around at Glass, really expecting an answer, but it was obvious that Glass just wasn't with him at the moment. He appeared to be in deep thought and Buck figured it didn't have a thing to do with the task at hand.

Buck had been right, because at that minute Glass was wondering how his latest batch of home-brew was coming in the basement of his home in Seattle. On one of his recent patrols some of the freshly bottled brew had done a little exploding. His wife, Joyce, hadn't appreciated it a bit! Not only was the popping of the bottles a source of concern for her, but the subsequent smell and mess had cooled their last welcome home together. Right now he was hoping that his last batch was behaving itself and staying in its respective bottles as the recipe stated. Beer-making had become a recent hobby of his and he thought if this worked out as it was supposed to, he might even try a batch of wine next time. After all, he had already invested in a great deal of equipment, and he liked wine almost as well as he did beer. Maybe he could even interest Joyce in some of that, since she hadn't shown much interest in his beer-making ability.

"What are you doing?" Buck asked, "spending liberty time in Anchorage before we even get there?"

"Eh, what do you mean?" Glass replied, as he tried desperately to bring his thoughts back to the task at hand.

"Oh, I didn't mean anything. You just looked like you were already in Anchorage, at least in thought anyway."

"As a matter of fact," Glass said, "I was home making another batch of home-brew. Either that or I was cleaning up the mess that the last batch made in our basement."

"Say, that reminds me," Buck mumbled as he put strain on another of the terminal screws, "you never have let me try any of your stuff. After all, as much beer as I drink I should be some kind of an authority."

"Shucks, kid, you're just a rank amateur at beer drinking," Glass shot back. "If you really want to see a beer drinker, you should meet that father-in-law of mine sometime! I'll bet he has spilled more beer than you ever saw, let alone drank."

Glass could see that the kid had been bothered a bit by the snappy way he had answered him, and he really hadn't meant to hurt his feelings, so he added, "Don't worry, I'll give you a couple bottles out of the new batch I have working at home." With that he gave Buck a half smile and a pat on the shoulder.

This was enough to bring Buck's confidence back, and he said, "O.K. I'll hold you to it as soon as we reach Seattle. I suppose we'll be spending a lot of time together when we get back. After all, I would imagine it'll be up to us to replace all this burned-out gear."

"No, I don't think they'll be expecting us to do the job," Glass replied. "It would just tie the ship up for quite a spell if they did. It's just too big for the two of us. I'm sure they'll have some contractor come in and do the whole thing. I would guess that they'll want at least one of us on the scene while it's being done, though."

The words had barely got out when the ship took a lurch over as she turned onto a new course. Both men made a grab for their beer bottles as well as something to keep their footing.

"What the hell is that helmsman trying to do, make our work harder than it already is?" Buck said, trying to retrieve the screwdriver that he had abandoned in favor of saving his beer.

"They just changed hands at the wheel," Glass said without knowing for sure. "You know this tub is pretty hard to hold on a straight course even when you know what you are doing. That plus the fact that we're up here quite a ways and every motion of the ship is exaggerated."

With that both men went back to their work not the least bit aware that the ship had really changed course and they were no longer headed toward Anchorage.

3. THE CHASE

To Captain Bruno A. Forsterer things were rather humdrum on the bridge of the *Wachusett* that morning. He had been on deck since 6 a.m. unable to sleep. He, like the enlisted men, was looking forward to the docking at Anchorage. Maybe not for the same reason, but nevertheless, looking forward to it. It would give him a chance to get his mail from home as well as get a couple of letters off to his wife. He had always found it difficult to write letters while out on a cruise. It just seemed so useless. After all, they couldn't be mailed until they reached port, and by the time he was able to mail them he would, no doubt, have some questions to answer when he received the mail from her.

His wife Patricia seemed to understand and was willing to go along with it. "Good gosh," he mumbled to himself, "she knows me well enough after being married for nearly 20 years to go along with the program." Yes, now that he thought about it they had been married in 1953, and that was about four years before he had gone to Officer Candidate School. As a matter of fact, she had been largely responsible for his making the choice. He had been a first-class quartermaster working in the Rescue Co-ordination Center in San Francisco at the time. It had meant moving to New London, Connecticut, and her living in some pretty shabby quarters for a time, but he had never regretted the move.

The watch officers well knew the captain's habit of appearing on the bridge during the early morning hours. They realized it was mainly to check on the progress made during the night, and to be sure everything was in order for the coming day. However, this morning it had been a little earlier than usual. It was rather obvious to them the captain was not in one of his better moods—there just seemed to be something in the air that gave him the appearance of being uneasy. He didn't normally stand on the sideline with absolutely nothing to say, but this morning that was exactly what he was doing.

Completely oblivious to those around him, the captain stood thinking of the 26 years he had served in the Coast Guard and of the several ships he had commanded prior to assuming command of the *Wachusett* about a year ago. During those years he had had premonitions that everything was not as it should be. It was that eerie feeling with no foundation in fact that he occasionally experienced. There usually wound up being a reason for it, but in the meantime there was very little he could do about it. Yes, he could remember the feeling when he was aboard the buoy tenders *Woodrush* and *Sassafras*, as commanding officer, and on those occasions either they developed engine trouble or received an emergency call following his feelings of unrest.

After nearly four hours of standing on the bridge with little or nothing to do except try to dispel the feeling, he finally gave up and informed Ensign Jefferson, who was serving as officer-of-the-deck on that watch, that he was going to his cabin, the captain then promptly left the bridge.

He tried stretching out on his bunk in an effort to pick up a few minutes' nap, but sleep would not come. After trying to force sleep on himself for a time, he gave up and swung his feet to the deck of the cabin. He picked up a book that he really did not want to read, but unlike the sleep, he thought he could force himself to do it.

This effort, too, was wasted. After scanning several pages he found that although he had been reading words, the meaning was just not penetrating, so he gave that up too, and just lay back waiting until what was going to happen did happen.

He found himself wondering what type of assignments he could pass on to the four cadets he had aboard. After all, he reasoned when they put them aboard the *Wachusett* from the Coast Guard Academy, they were expected to be given duties that would provide an insight into the operation of a cutter. He had given them junior-officer-of-the-deck tasks, and had on occasion allowed them to make courtesy boardings of foreign vessels. They had performed well on each occasion—but what was there left for them to observe or take part in?

"Oh, hell," he told himself, "what a silly thing to be worrying about. I would be far better off concerning myself with 'Albie' and his capers." "Albie" was the nickname he and his wife had tied on his son, Bruno A. Forsterer III. Evidently the boy was a real chip off the old block; now 11 years old, he was giving his mother a few difficult moments. When he wasn't heckling other children in school he was heckling his younger sister Sally. For a while he thought he could snap the boy into line—but he had to admit seeing the family occasionally was not the real answer.

He had no idea how long he had lain there when activity in the radio room—located directly across from his cabin—brought him to the realization that something unusual was happening.

He quickly brought his six-foot-four-inch frame up out of the bunk and strode across to the radio room. Walking through the hatch doors had always been somewhat of a problem. Even though a door might accommodate his height he had bumped his head enough that he automatically stooped as he entered or left a room. He hadn't given the matter that much thought before but had to admit it might be one of the contributing factors to his trim stature.

"What's up?" he asked the radio operator as he entered the room.

"It's an inquiry as to our position," the radioman answered, adding, "by the station at Kodiak."

"Well, I'm going up to the bridge again, so I'll get it for you and send the information back for them." As he said it he turned and left for the ladder that would take him to the bridge.

On reaching the top step he noticed that the weather had not changed; there was still a fine mist and spray hitting the ports across the front of the ship.

The request for position was not uncommon; it was the duty of the Coast Guard stations up and down the coast to keep close tabulation as to where vessels were, in the event they were needed for some rescue tasks, one of the prime reasons the U.S. Coast Guard was in existence.

The captain seems to be a little on edge thought Lt. jg Jones as he quickly plotted their position and passed it on to the boatswain's mate to take to the radio operator. Possibly he was worrying about his boy in school. He had mentioned that he was eager to get his mail and see how things were going at home. Anyway, they would be in Anchorage in a few hours and everything would be fine.

The messenger had hardly left before he returned with another message, this one informing them that they should stand by for a change of orders. A message like that could only mean they were getting an assignment that would be in another direction from the one they had been traveling.

Captain Forsterer was leaning against the bulkhead on the starboard side, his blue eyes staring straight ahead, apparently deep in thought. The message directed them to reverse course and head for 155 degrees west longitude and 55 degrees north latitude, which would take them back over some waters they had been traveling. The message carried no reason for the sudden change but indicated there would be more coming shortly. It brought wrinkles to the captain's forehead as he had been eagerly looking forward to receiving his mail. This could well mean a delay of one, two or even three days in their arrival at Anchorage.

"It looks like it could be a busy morning," he said. "Better send for Radioman Walton—we'll probably need the additional hand in the radio room if we are going to get all this straight."

Jones merely turned around to the messenger and instructed him to find Sparks, as Radioman Joel Walton was known to all members of the crew.

Jones glanced at the captain out of the corner of his eye. He expected there would be some speculation as to what the emergency was, but he dropped the thought of starting any such conversation as he heard Captain Forsterer rather gruffly inform the helmsman to slow engines. He seemed to be having a mental argument with himself before issuing the order to come about. It was as though for at least one full minute he had considered ignoring the order. At other times the captain had seemed pleased if not thrilled at the thought of his ship being needed for whatever purpose the command station might have.

"Old 44" listed more than usual. As the turn was half completed, she had dropped into a trough midway through. She quickly righted herself, though, as they moved into the next wave. The sea was now following them, which made going much easier.

The helmsman noticed the touch of gruffness in the captain's voice but figured what the hell. The old man hadn't had to handle the wheel for so many years he didn't remember what a pain it could be. His mind was so far from what he was actually doing that he did not realize he had started swinging the wheel hard to starboard before observing the wave movement a little better. The result was that he had barely started the maneuver when the ship slipped into the trough between two waves and began listing heavily. He actually looked over in the captain's direction half expecting a slight reprimand for the lack of foresight.

Fire Controlman First Class Fred Glass standing near bow of Cutter *Wachusett*. Glass was one of the two Coast Guardsmen who brought the Japanese gillnetter *Jinmei Maru* into Kodiak after interception. Inset: Night picture of the *Wachusett* as it appeared in a Seattle shipyard being refitted before the Alaskan cruise. (Photos courtesy U.S. Coast Guard and Lt. Cmdr. Robert H. Stracener)

Commander Bruno Forsterer

Forsterer commanded the *Wachusett* during the eventful Alaskan cruise.

Lt. Commander Robert H. Stracener

Stracener, with Glass, brought the Japanese gillnetter *Jinmei Maru* into Kodiak after interception.

Photos courtesy
U.S. Coast Guard

His quick glance told him the captain was not only positioned for the heavy list of the vessel, but also must have been a million miles away in thought. When the ship had righted herself and was now headed with the wind, the young man at the wheel turned his thoughts to other things. At least, he thought, steaming in this direction he could turn off that infernal swish-swishing of the windshield wipers. They always had bugged him. As he stood there twisting the wheel from one side to the other trying to maintain a steady course, those damned wipers had a way of hypnotizing him, and there had been several occasions when he had caught himself half asleep while on watch because of them.

Everyone on the bridge came out of their reverie as the latest message was brought up from the radio room: Four Japanese fishing ships had been sighted in the area into which they were now moving and it would be up to them to lend any assistance to the Coast Guard aircraft that was maintaining observation."

"How far away from us are they located, Mr. Jones?" the captain asked, scowling at the message he had been handed.

The captain hadn't called him Mr. Jones with such emphasis on the "Mr." since he first came aboard over a year ago Jones recalled as he answered, "I have it figured going full tilt some place between 20 and 25 hours."

"Pass that information on to Kodiak. Maybe they will reconsider our heading back that way," the captain shouted; then in a quieter voice cancelled it out with, "Oh, hell, they know where we are and what our speed is so let it go. I just hope it isn't some damned wild goose chase. Those Japanese could be half way back to Japan by the time we get there if they are so inclined."

"There is the possibility they're not aware of the fact they have been observed," Jones volunteered. "They may not even know that they are in illegal waters and will just continue fishing."

"Hell, if I know those airdales they will have to get down pretty low to determine that they are Japanese," the captain shot back.

"Do you want me to tell them our expected time of arrival at the site, just on the off chance they haven't figured it out?" Jones asked.

"No, let's let it go for the time being," was the answer. "We should be hearing something more pretty directly I would think."

It was obvious to Jones that the captain was warming up to the task as he no longer had the strained tone in his voice and appeared to be more his old self. Jones, who had ambitions to become a career officer in the Guard, had held the ship's commander in high esteem since first coming aboard the *Wachusett.*

"See what you can do about plotting the best possible course. Maybe we can shave some time off your estimate by using this following sea as long as we can," the captain said with some enthusiasm. "We just might see a little action before this cruise is over."

Jones really didn't need any encouragement. He had already pulled the charts out and was trying to determine the best course to steer. After figuring and re-figuring various courses, he made his decision.

Turning around from the plotting board he said, "I do believe if we take advantage of the wind and following sea until we get to this point," pointing to one of the charts, "we could possibly bring our time down closer to 20 hours, unless we happen to hit heavy seas after making the swing to the south."

"Ask Kodiak what the condition of the seas are in the area," the captain replied, "and give them the estimated time of arrival." He wanted to tell him to ask that they be kept posted on what was going on, but figured they would do that when and if they saw fit, and his asking for it wasn't going to change anything anyway.

Jones gave orders to the helmsman on the course he wanted and appeared to enjoy the new atmosphere that was now prevalent in the pilothouse.

"Old 44" seemed to feel the urgent need to hurry and was slicing through the water faster than usual for her age and power.

Kodiak sent back a report that seas were only fair in the area of the fishing fleet, adding that the Coast guard aircraft had advised the Japanese they should pull up their nets and proceed to Kodiak—but as of the last report the request was being ignored.

This report brought spirits even higher on the bridge of the *Wachusett,* what with the ship appearing to be straining herself to leap faster through the water, and the fact that the aircraft were attempting to send the fishing fleet in their direction.

With the last report, Captain Forsterer decided that his continued presence on the bridge was unnecessary. "I'll be in my cabin if you need me," he said with a wave of his hand as he started down the ladder to his quarters. In any case, he would be closer to the radio room and could keep far better track of what was going on. As far as the bridge was concerned there was little doubt the crew would do their level best to get them on the scene as soon as possible.

The strain of the last few minutes was starting to be felt as he slowly descended, but now he knew why he again had that funny feeling and again it had proved correct.

As he neared the radio room door, he realized that the Kodiak Coast Guard Station had to be pretty busy themselves that morning. They were putting out calls not only to the Buoy Tender *Citrus*, which had recently left that port, but also to the ice breaker *Burton Island* and the Tender *Clover*. After carefully analyzing the messages, he determined that the *Burton Island* had been steaming north and would be in position to intercept the fishermen, if they continued heading southerly. The *Citrus* and the *Clover* were both in position farther north than the *Wachusett* and therefore chances were good they could cut off any escape in that direction. The *Burton Island*, as the southernmost of the cutters, had a good chance of intercepting a continued flight in that direction. By all indications these fishermen were trapped and it would just be a question of which Coast Guard vessel they would be forced to give up to. It would be their speed and direction that would answer that question. He was just hopeful that they would be the one. Now that they had been alerted and invited into the action, they would like to get something out of it besides lost liberty time.

Messages being intercepted between the Coast Guard C-130 patrol plane and Kodiak indicated that the fishing boats were continuing their flight in a southerly direction, putting the *Wachusett* in the best possible position—but depending a great deal on the speed of the fishing boats.

The C-130 had indicated that three Japanese fishermen had got underway after cutting from one to three miles of gill nets loose. The boats were described as having orange hulls with red trim and deckhouse. All three were seen to have salmon on deck as well as salmon in their nets. The plan at that time was that air surveillance would be maintained until the cutters could intercept the violators.

The *Wachusett* and the *Clover* were the only cutters officially dispatched to intercept at this point but the *Citrus* and the *Burton Island* had been told to be prepared to enter the action if needed. With fingers crossed, Captain Forsterer left the radiomen to their work and walked the width of the passageway to his own cabin, deciding to let fate take its course.

One thing foremost on his mind, as he sat down on the bunk, was his hope that the aircraft did not lose contact with the fishermen. With the weather being nasty as it was and the aircraft forced to relieve each other because of fuel problems, there was always the possibility of losing sight of the poachers. To lose them once in the fog could mean days trying to find them again—and a good possibility they could get away altogether.

4. SETTING THE TRAP

By now the word had filtered down to the mess hall, and the enthusiasm exhibited on the bridge became contagious for the men, too, were showing signs of eagerness to get to the scene in time for some type of action. They had no idea at the time what the action might prove to be; nevertheless most looked forward to any kind of encounter, hoping it would break the monotony. So, they had boarded a few foreign fishing vessels in the past and had inspected their fishing gear for possible illegal fishing, but they had never made an arrest that any of them, even the oldest hands aboard, could recall.

Speculation continued for the balance of the day and evening as reports were relayed down that aircraft were keeping a close watch on the fleet. Now, instead of there being three Japanese fishing boats, it was learned that there was a fourth and they were spread out approximately 10 miles apart. The fleet apparently was still making a serious attempt to run for it, but their lack of speed was in the *Wachusett's* favor. Yes, they felt there was still hope of overhauling them. The feeling was that as long as the props continued running at full speed there was chance of a little excitement.

As the afternoon wore on, word was passed that aircraft had descended close to the water beside the fishing fleet and dropped canisters explaining in both English and Japanese that the four vessels were fishing in U.S. territorial waters and they were to proceed immediately to Kodiak. The Japanese had turned about after reading the messages, but as soon as the aircraft had left the immediate area had taken a new tack toward the south. Messages indicated that when the fourth vessel was sighted they had tarps draped over the bow blocking off the ship's registration number. In addition to that, they had tarps draped over the stern hiding from view the ship's name. To further complicate identification, they had hidden the markings on the bridge and stack of the vessel. It was only the tarps flapping in the breeze that made identification possible. This news added considerably to wiping out any fear the crew might have had that they were just on another "wild goose chase" that would interrupt their liberty.

"Hell," Boatswain's Mate Hughes said, "as long as we are going to be sitting around here waiting for the latest news, we might as well be playing some poker."

"What for?" piped someone from the back, "you already have about all the money on this tub. You even have a fortune in I.O.U.'s. So many in fact that no one is going to have much of a liberty when and if we ever do get to Anchorage."

"What do you want to do, just sit around picking your damned nose?"

That was about all that was needed because a deck of cards came to life out of nowhere and the game was on even though someone mentioned that they would have to clear the tables soon for the evening chow.

The players moved to the back of one of the long tables and the game started. Some of the crew, not the least interested in the game, moved into the chow line and found other places to sit rather than disturb the players. Of course, there was some grumbling, but no more than usual.

After the tables had been cleared of trays used for the meal, poker games sprouted out all over the room. The changing of the watch brought new information as well as more men seeking food.

Word passed fast among those in the mess hall that a helicopter equipped with loud speaker and Japanese interpreter had been dispatched to the fishing fleet. Like the others, it met with little or no success. Even though the chopper had hovered slightly above the vessels the men had gone about their work as though it didn't exist. An attempt to put a boarding party aboard one of them had also proved a worthless venture, when it was found that the seas were too high to risk the lives of those who would be boarding. That the Japanese fishermen were either deaf and dumb or darned good actors was the consensus as the poker games continued.

When the discussion surrounding present conditions with respect to the Japanese had begun to fade, one of the crew members peering out a porthole said, "It must be miserable weather here most of the time," not talking to anyone in particular, "but it does stay light rather late even though you can rarely see the sun."

"Well, just hope that we meet those Japanese in the daylight. They don't appear to be too eager to go to Kodiak."

"Yeh, isn't that the truth," someone said, adding, "say, Glass did you fellows ever get that fire control junk working? Or will we have to throw rocks at them when and if we catch them?"

"No," Glass replied, "we did get the wires pulled enough, though, so that gun can be fired manually, and what the hell, just the boom should scare them into going to Kodiak with us."

"You fellows don't have to worry about meeting those Japanese in the dark," Glass continued. "We have moved eight boxes of 81mm mortar illumination shells into the upper handling room, so if we catch up with them we'll be able to make our own daylight. You guys know there are three shells each in those cases, and eight cases should go a long way toward scaring hell· out of them and making our own sunshine."

"Sure that worked out fine when we used them on that clown who was rowing to Hawaii, but what happens when you shoot one of those things up through the clouds—and don't tell me we don't have some mighty low clouds," came a response from somewhere in the room.

"Hell, we were firing those for the maximum height of 15,000 feet, but we can control how high they go by adjusting the tail fins. They can be adjusted, and the degree of tilt on the tail fin determines how high they go," Glass shot back at whoever had come up with the statement.

One of the poker players reached for his billfold as he remarked, "It's funny that you should bring that clown up. I received a news clipping from my girl friend in our last mail about that incident. It was supposed to have been in the *Seattle Times* recently."

"You trying to tell us that you have a girl friend?" someone piped up.

"Aw, be quiet. I want to hear what they had to say about it," another of the players came back.

"Well, somebody wrote in to this guy 'Troubleshooter' and asked how much money that affair cost the taxpayers. He says the thing cost a total of $31,200. Not too shabby, eh?"

"How in the hell did they come up with a figure like that? Does it say?"

"Well, it says here, 'To locate and rescue Mr. Quesnel after he issued a distress call 970 miles from Hawaii took 9.6 hours flight time with a C-130 aircraft at a cost of $6,400 and 96 hours steaming by the cutter *Wachusett* at a cost of $12,000.' Then down a little farther it says, 'In addition a previous Coast Guard search off the coast of California and the evacuation of one of Mr. Quesnel's rowing partners cost an additional $10,300.' "

"Boy, the cost of a couple of guys in a C-130 sure runs into money in comparison to what they put down as the cost of operating this cutter. Hell, the aircraft was only up less than 10 hours and cost damned near as much money as it did for us to operate for close to 100 hours. Just doesn't make good sense."

"I'll tell you it seemed like a whale of a lot more than 96 hours that we were out there looking for that cat."

"Aw, come on, deal the cards," another of the players chimed in.

"Just hold your water, I want to hear this," said the guardsman who had made the first inquiry.

"Aw, come on, do you want to play cards or start a gossip column?"

That remark was completely ignored as the first went through the motions of shuffling the cards saying, "Hell, that still doesn't add up to $31,200 the way I figure it."

"No, it doesn't, but it goes on here to say that there was a cost of administration for processing the case of some $500, and that makes the grand total of $31,200."

"Here, let me see that article. I want to read it when this hand is over," the dealer said passing out the cards to the players, who seemed to be showing little or no interest in the entire conversation as they concentrated on their cards.

"The only thing I can say about the whole mess is that they should have had some of those figures when we brought him into Seattle. Maybe then they wouldn't have made such a celebrity out of him," remarked someone from the sidelines.

"Boy you can say that again. They sure as hell weren't treating him as though he had cost anyone any money then," another said.

"Sure a crazy, mixed up world," said one of the players who had been pushing for the poker game to continue.

"Say, Glass, didn't you say you guys moved some illumination shells to the upper handling room?" one of the players asked by way of changing the subject. "If so, that must mean that they think we will be catching those poachers sometime tonight."

One of the fellows shortly off watch replied, "Well, I think they were figuring if the fishing boats head back like they were told, or even if they stay dead in the water, we should be catching them sometime tonight. But on the other hand, it will be sometime tomorrow before we will see them, unless, of course, they are capable of outrunning us and at this stage of the game there's just no way of knowing what's happening."

"Shit, if those fishing boats have any speed at all they ought to be able to keep outa range until they're a few miles from Japan and then what're we supposed to do?"

"We'll miss our liberty in Anchorage, that's what we'll do," volunteered one of the players.

Another of those who had just come off watch shot back with, "We don't have to worry about chasing them all the way to Japan because the ice breaker *Burton Island* is supposed to be out beyond the fishing boats moving into position to intercept 'em if they outrun us an the *Citrus*."

"Well, that's some consolation," was the reply. "At least we won't have to run all the way across the Pacific."

"I don't know how much good the *Citrus* is. They can't go half as fast as we can, and it's doubtful whether we can catch them or not."

"They have to let the local boys get in on the glory some way."

"Maybe they deserve some of it. After all, how would you like to have to live up here all the time?" was another comment.

A radioman recently off watch moved over into one of the aisles and said, "Say, did you fellows hear that the guys on the *Citrus* really put up a fuss when they were called away from their girl friends at Kodiak? It seems the headquarters figured they could handle the whole mess without getting us involved at the beginning."

"It looks to me like they're trying to justify having more aircraft, and doing away with as many surface craft as possible. But if they do have to settle for some surface craft being involved in this caper, it's going to be the local boys you can bet," another volunteered.

"As far as I'm concerned, anything that these guys stationed up here can get they deserve. I sure as hell wouldn't want to live here. Seattle is bad enough."

"You can say that again," someone else chimed in, adding, "I believe duty up here would just about compare with anything on the East Coast. There is another lousy place to have to be stationed."

"Ah, quit bitching. At least when this is over we can take our liberty in Anchorage and then head for home and that's about all I'm interested in at this point." Tossing his hand he added, "It's a cinch, I'm not doing a damned bit of good playing cards."

"What's the matter, you getting tired of the pleasant company of your shipmates?" someone laughingly asked.

"You bet your sweet butt I'm getting tired of seeing your crummy mugs." Then he turned and said, "Come on, Glass, you can have my seat here if you want to make yourself a fortune in the game."

"You know what you can do with that seat of yours," Glass shot back, declaring, "You know I don't care one hop in hell about playing cards of any kind, but if you want to get the chess board out we can talk business."

"To hell with you and your chess," was the reply. "Besides, I'm ready for that old fart sack. I'm tired, and don't anyone say, what from?"

"What the heck's your hurry?" Hughes asked, "I don't have all your money yet."

"That isn't all. I don't plan on letting you get it all."

"There is always tomorrow night," someone else volunteered, knowing that what Hughes didn't win tonight he would probably win some other time.

5. "FULL SPEED AHEAD"

Captain Forsterer felt fairly well rested as he pulled himself from his bunk the next morning. He didn't know why but he had half expected to be roused from his sleep before now. He had left word on the bridge to call him if anything out of the ordinary happened. He could remember waking two or three times during the night, but after determining no one was around he proceeded to fall back into a half sleep. It hadn't troubled him a great deal because he had always been a light sleeper, and accustomed to opening one eye at any unusual noise.

As he splashed water on his face and looked into the mirror he realized that there had been little chance they would catch up with the fishing fleet during the night, unless of course, they were to heed the warning they had received and stop. He had rationalized the night before that if they hadn't observed the stop order while the planes were overhead it was very unlikely the orders would mean much to them when planes were not in their midst. It was pretty apparent now that they didn't intend to stop until they were forced to.

He could still envision one of the radio communications that had gone out of the Coast Guard Headquarters in Juneau destined for headquarters in Washington, D.C. He especially recalled the parts that pertained to his ship: "CGC *Wachusett* and CGC *Clover* diverted to scene." Then there was the part, "Intercept and board JA VSLS." The part about "Violation confirmed by boarding, detain and escort VSLS to Kodiak pending delivery to JA authorities" didn't concern him as much as he thought it should. He just couldn't visualize the Japanese destroying evidence, so the confirming bit didn't seem necessary. After all, the aircraft had photographed the vessels with nets out and fish on their decks; that should be evidence enough for anyone. Of course the Japanese did have the entire night to dump their catch if they really did expect to be caught. He was still betting they thought escape was not only possible but almost a certainty.

There was no point in brooding about the situation, he told himself. He had been informed that the *Burton Island* was moving into position on the Japanese west flank to cut them off if they persisted in running. He knew with the first light the C-130's would be out there plotting a course for the best interception. Of course, the Japanese would have no way of knowing that they were boxed in; that information would not come out until Coast Guard cutters started appearing as pips on their radar screen. Even then the Japanese could not know they were anything but another fishing vessel. The only problem he figured he had at that moment was to decide whether to eat breakfast in his cabin or have it sent to the bridge. He decided the latter would be the best move. In that way the watch could brief him on what, if anything, had happened during the few hours that he had been sleeping and he would be able to pass orders to cope with coming events that much quicker. There was a good possibility that these events would have a lasting impression on a great many people, in both the United States and Japan. Yes, the matter was going to take a whole lot of finesse to complete satisfactorily.

As he sat down on the edge of the bunk lacing his shoes, he recalled that he had already informed Lt. Stracener he would be heading up the first boarding crew if it became necessary. Now as he kicked the order around in his mind he was sure he had made the right choice. The lieutenant was Operations Officer on this cruise and deserving of the recognition. On the other hand, he had to admit to himself that he had been riding the junior officer a bit lately, but he felt some justification. If the lieutenant was ever to become anything besides a junior officer, he would have to be able to cope with such things and still maintain his "cool." It all went with being a commanding officer in any branch of the military service.

He only hoped that he had impressed on the lieutenant enough the need to be strict in the enforcement of orders after taking command of the first fishing boat. It was his intention to seize more than one of the offenders if possible, and he certainly didn't want to worry about what was taking place on the first vessel after it had once been secured. He would like to be able just to forget the first one and concentrate on catching the second, but he knew that would be impossible in the true sense of the word.

Actually, if he could have his way he would capture all four, but without some sort of miracle that was highly unlikely. However, the thought still brought a slight smile to his lips. One of the things that really concerned him was the order that had been passed down from Coast Guard headquarters, a few weeks ago, spelling out that when prize crews were put aboard any foreign vessel the cutter placing such crews should remain within view of that vessel at all times until the crew could be removed or relieved.

He knew that the order had been the result of an incident involving a Russian fishing fleet in the Bering Sea. This event— which had made little impression at the time—had happened in late January: the ice breaker *Storis*, on routine patrol, had discovered the 362-foot *Lamut*, and the 278-foot trawler *Kolyvan* 9-1/2 miles off St. Matthew Island, about 2-1/2 miles inside U.S. waters. The two vessels were boarded by the Coast Guard while they were moored together. It had seemed simple enough at the time, but things hadn't gone too well since.

The *Storis* then ordered both Soviet vessels to head for Adak Island, a naval station 600 miles south in the Aleutians. According to reports, the journey had barely begun when both Soviet vessels stopped, saying they would go no farther. There had been considerable delay before negotiations brought a resumption of movement. But the *Lamut*, carrying fleet Commander Vladimir Artemov, suddenly broke away, carrying with it the prize crew from the *Storis*.

For the next four hours, the *Storis* chased the *Lamut*, having received permission from Coast Guard headquarters to fire if they felt it was necessary. It had been learned later that the boarding party had been crowded into a corner and were unable to stop the race. At the end, the *Storis* kept crossing the Russian's bow. The maneuvering forced the Russian to change course, thus slowing him down. They had been in ice and the

Storis had an advantage because it was an icebraker. Finally, the *Storis* ordered him to stop or he would be forced to take action. When he warned that he was ready to fire, the Russian decided he had gone far enough. The problem had been that the boarding crew on the trawler had completely lost touch with the icebreaker and a rendezvous had been questionable for a time. Things had worked out satisfactorily in the end, but the affair had made future boardings to be viewed as anything but routine.

Captain Forsterer could well imagine himself in the same position in respect to the Japanese vessels he was presently chasing, although he did have one thing to his advantage. The *Storis* had been involved in the incident without any other cutters in the immediate vicinity, while the *Wachusett* had help available in the form of aircraft as well as three other cutters. Still, with the attitude the Japanese were taking, ignoring aircraft instructions, anything would be possible when they met.

As the captain pulled his jacket on, he reasoned that he had picked the right man in Lt. Stracener. The man was far more religious than he himself was and therefore more likely to avoid violence than perhaps another officer.

The radio room didn't seem to be over active as he passed on his way to the bridge. As he started up the ladder at the end of the passage, his thoughts went back to Lt. Stracener. He had allowed the lieutenant to pick the three enlisted men who would be accompanying him on the boarding. He only hoped that the lieutenant would be very careful in his selection. They would have to be men with some experience, but certainly men who would respond immediately to an order if an emergency developed. He felt he had done the right thing in allowing Stracener to pick the people who would accompany him, but could he be that sure the lieutenant would consider all angles in his choice of men?

Oh, hell, he reasoned, the choice has been made now, and I'm sure as I can be that it was right. Maybe, though, he should be more concerned about his choice for the second boarding party. He remembered granting Ensign Mike Conway that task. True, the ensign had asked for the assignment, and it wasn't run-of-the-mill procedure to grant such requests; after all, Lieutenant Charles Jones had also asked for that chore, but it just seemed like the right thing to do at the time. He was convinced that if there was to be any resistance it would come from the first seizure rather than the second, so he didn't feel the risk of assigning a real junior officer as all that important.

"Good morning, gentlemen," the captain said as he entered the pilothouse—more to let them know that he was present than as a greeting. Both Ensign Bartley and Lt. Jones answered at the same time, almost as though they had been rehearsing during the morning watch.

Without being asked, Lt. Jones volunteered the information that they were not expecting to come within radar range of at least one of the fishing boats for a couple of hours.

The captain noticed that lookouts stationed on both the port and starboard wings were busy scanning the waters in front of the ship.

"It doesn't appear as though the weather has improved any during the night," mused the captain, and with the same breath, "Ask the messenger to go down and bring up some coffee, please."

With a quick "Aye, aye, sir," the messenger was gone as though glad to be out of the area, at least for the time being. He had heard both Jones and Bartley discussing their desire to head up one of the boarding parties and their dissatisfaction with the two officers who had been picked. He also knew that the captain would be reluctant to hear any suggestions that the orders be changed. He doubted that either of them would be very happy with the results of a change. As he reached the bottom of the ladder and headed aft down one of the passageways, he reasoned that they felt someone else has already been picked for the job. They should know by now that the captain was still running the ship.

"I don't expect my assignments to be questioned!" the messenger overheard as he returned with the pot of coffee and three cups. Apparently one or both officers had approached the captain with their desire for an assignment change, and the captain had let them know there would be no changing.

"Would you ask Mr. Pearson to join me on the bridge?" looking squarely at the messenger the captain was beyond a doubt closing conversation as to what officer or officers would receive that assignment.

As he issued the order, Captain Forsterer could rememer when he first came out of Officer Candidate School. There had been a great many things that he had wanted to do and it hadn't taken a great deal of time to find out that it wasn't necessarily what you wanted to do in this outfit—you did what you were told to do. Every new officer was expected to put in his apprenticeship and you didn't complete it by doing what you damn well pleased.

He had waited his turn. He had spent 11 years working up through the ranks to first-class quartermaster before he even had the chance to attend O.C.S. and he had done a great many chores that were not to his liking while a junior officer, and he thought of himself as being the better for it.

Just how in hell did they expect him to maintain any type of discipline on this ship if he allowed anyone to question his orders, he asked himself as he poured a cup of coffee and took a large swallow.

As the darkness started giving way to the gray he thought it would be a good time to lay out the course of action that would be taken. Some of the moves could be handled in advance of the actual encounter with the fishing fleet. He knew from experience that when things start happening, sometimes they happen so fast that you wish some previous preparations had been made.

"Mr. Jones, as soon as the morning mess is over I'm going to want the Gunner's Mates standing by their gun and I'm going to want some men in the magazine ready to pass up shells just in case they're needed. I also want the Signalmen on the ready because we're going to be using the signal lamp when we bring them in sight." With that the captain turned to Lt. jg Bartley.

"Are they bringing anything in on that radar yet?"

"Not as yet, sir, but we should be bringing something in soon," Bartley answered, then turned to stare straight forward again, feeling very uncomfortable. He knew he had another hour of watch left and that it would be one of the longest hours of his life. He wished to heavens he had left things alone and not mentioned the fact that he would like to head up one of the boarding parties. He had only meant to let the captain know that he would like the job, not that he was questioning his command. It was just another of the times he should have been listening rather than talking, he told himself, but even that didn't seem to be very consoling.

"Messenger, you better have my steward send my breakfast up here. I'm not going to have time to go below," the captain said.

He hadn't bothered to wait for the "Aye, aye, sir," but stepped out on the port wing and stood behind the lookout to get a breath of air and let some of the fine spray rinse his brow. He couldn't understand why he should be so up-tight but this morning it seemed that he was more than usually conscious of his command. He couldn't even remember how long it had been since he had felt so nervous but he had to admit to himself that "up-tight" he was.

"Did you wish to see me, Captain?"

"Oh, yes, Commander," Captain Forsterer said, a little startled. He hadn't realized that Lt. Cmdr. Pearson had moved out on the wing beside him. "I would like you to brief the men and officers of the first two boarding parties. We should be coming on one of those fellows in a few hours and I want the crews ready to jump on the first one fast so we have a chance at the rest before they get too far away. You better tell them to go easy on the rough stuff; we don't want any trouble if it can be avoided. Oh, hell, you know what to tell them."

The captain turned to ask if he had had his breakfast yet, but when he looked around, he found that Pearson had slipped away as quietly as he had materialized a few minutes before. Oh, well, he knew he didn't have to worry about Pearson impressing the men concerning no violence; he was good at that sort of thing. He strolled back into the pilothouse and started concentrating on the breakfast the messenger had set down for him.

The tray was on the edge of the chart table with a white napkin stretched over the top. He didn't have the vaguest idea what it contained, but wasn't too surprised to see that he had a couple of eggs, bacon and several pieces of toast. He hadn't thought of himself as hungry but did realize that if there was going to be action during the coming hours he had best get his eating done early—there would be no time for it later.

"What is the latest on the *Burton Island* and the *Citrus?*" he asked as he shoved the last of the toast into his mouth.

He hadn't put the question to anyone in particular, but he had expected Jones would answer, so he was a little surprised when Bartley offered the requested information.

"The *Burton Island* is moving south to intercept if they keep heading southwest as the last C-130 reports indicated. The *Citrus* is a little farther north than our present position and they will continue that course in case the fishermen change course in that direction. We should be getting our first morning reports from the aircraft any time now. They are supposed to be in the air."

"This waiting can get to a person," the captain said, again to no one in particular.

No one bothered to answer. Everyone on the bridge appeared to be busy with whatever it was they were doing.

6. "PREPARE FOR BOARDING"

It hadn't been long since the crew had completed breakfast when the ship's intercom started blatting, "Now hear this. Puderbaugh, Dennis, Kjiellin, Franklin, Dempsey and Glass, lay up to the Marine Science Tech Lab on the double!" The message was repeated three times with "Moose" Kjiellin and Glass just looking at each other in wonder as to what the message meant. Neither thought that it could be a disciplinary move because both felt they had been of good character, at least for the last few days.

"What do you suppose that's all about?" Moose asked turning to Glass.

"Your guess is just as good as mine," Glass replied. "I suppose the only way we are going to find out is go up and see what the man wants."

Both men fell silent as they headed down the passageway toward the midship location of the M.S.T. lab. There were several times that Glass was tempted to ask Moose what kind of trouble he had gotten himself into, but then realized that he was being called down as well, and it was a certainty he didn't have the vaguest idea what was going on.

As they stepped into the lab they noticed that the other fellows who had been called had already beaten them to the rendezvous. Each had the same puzzled look that Moose and Glass had.

The ship's Executive Officer Lt. Cmdr. Pearson was standing at one end of the lab, flanked by Lt. Stracener and Ensign Conway. All looked grim as they motioned for the six men to find a place where they could hear.

"You men have been picked to form the boarding parties that will go aboard the first and second Japanese fishing boats we encounter," Mr. Pearson said, continuing with what appeared to be a difficult speech he had quickly put together. "Stracener, Franklin, Dempsey and Glass will make up the first group, and Conway will head up the second group."

He looked around the room to see what impression his words had made, then went on, "Now we don't have any idea how long you fellows will be forced to stay aboard after seizing the boats, so I'm asking each of you to put a few things together for the trip. A change of clothes, shaving gear and whatever else you feel you will need. Now, I don't have any idea whether you will be asked to stay aboard one day or five; it depends on what type of cooperation we receive, but I can say it will be at least two days at the very least. We have been ordered to escort them into Kodiak if we find evidence they have been fishing illegally."

It sounded as though he was having difficulty bringing the words out as he continued, "I would like to point out that we want to avoid violence at all cost, when you go aboard. Just remember, at this point we are not positive of our action, and we certainly do not want to be the cause of an international incident." With that the Exec. took a deep breath before going on, "We have no idea how soon we will be contacting the first of the fleet, so I would suggest you men get right with it and put the things together you're going to need and report back here. Make sure you hold your needs to a minimum because there isn't going to be all that much room to take your entire sea bag. O.K., men, you are dismissed for the time being, but I'll expect you back here shortly." With that he turned and the three officers started conversing among themselves, cutting off any chance for questioning by the six enlisted men.

When the shock of surprise wore off the six, they turned and slowly left the lab, each trying to figure why they had been picked for the assignment.

Glass just couldn't believe the feeling of finality that gripped him as he headed for his locker. There was no reason to believe that anything serious was about to take place as far as he was concerned but the feeling persisted.

He reluctantly pulled the small flight bag from his locker and unzipped it on a nearby bench. As he turned to grab his electric razor he glanced up to the picture he had on the inside door.

Unlike most of the Coasties, he didn't have an assortment of pin-up pictures adorning the inside of his locker door; he had a picture of his wife, Joyce. In the picture she was bending down with her arms around their son "Mike" and of course their dog "Queenie" was seated in front of them both. He really couldn't recall seeing as much in that picture before as he did now.

Queenie was getting to be rather old now, but he remembered when he and his wife had gone to the "dog pound" in Norfolk, Virginia, and picked the little puppy out. He had been as much responsible for the idea as Joyce at the time. He was getting things in shape to leave for the next nine months. That was just before leaving on the "SS-580," the submarine *Bar Bell*. That was when they were starting "West Pak," which would prove to be a tour nearly around the world, visiting ports from the Near East to the Far East. He had thought the dog would prove to be a protection and companion for her while he was gone. By now it had become just like another member of the family.

He managed to get the razor into the flight bag but as he turned to pick up an extra pair of dungarees his eyes went back to the picture. There was Joyce smiling out at him, and he had to admit to himself that he really loved that little girl. They had met while both were going to Navy school at Bainbridge, Maryland. He had been attending Fire Control school while she was taking "boot" training and studying to be a communications technician. They had dated and gone to many dances during the time and continued to see a great deal of each other during the next year before getting married in Washington, D.C.

As he tore his eyes away from the picture, a funny feeling gripped him. He jammed the dungarees into the bag and turned back to the locker for a couple of additional pairs of sox. In spite of himself, his eyes went back to the picture and the thought raced through his mind of the time the two of them had gone fishing. Joyce had worn dress clothing for the occasion, indicating to him that she didn't know a great deal about fishing. However, he had an old pair of boots in the car that he made her put on to protect her sandals. When she had stumbled down the path to the water's edge in those boots he had tagged her with a nickname. To him she was thereafter known as "Humphrey" because she reminded him so much of the character in the Joe Palooka comic strip. No, she hadn't liked the name too well, but she was a good sport and went along with it. That was just the way she always was; if it was something to make him happy, she was all for it. She and Mike were enough to make any man's life worth living. Now, there was a super-boy for you. Mike was a son to be really proud of. And to top it all, the chances were good that Joyce would be able to carry through her present pregnancy after having bad luck with several. Yep, Fred Glass, he mused, you really have been a lucky devil.

He continued to stuff articles into the bag, thinking of the many places they had lived together before their son Mike had joined the family. They had been stationed in Pearl Harbor, Norfolk, Va., Great Lakes, Ill., Dam Neck, Va., and San Diego, Calif. before he went aboard one of the newest nuclear submarines, the *Lewis and Clark*, in 1966. It had been shortly after that he had decided to leave the service, believing they could have a better life if he was home more. Taking a job with Burroughs and later I.B.M. had only kept him away from home more than the submarine service so they decided that he should continue his service career. This time he had tried the Coast Guard. Now, here he was wondering why he had this feeling of apprehension and if this could perhaps be the end of the line.

Glass found it extremely hard to swallow as he closed the locker and turned to zip the bag closed. He didn't even want to look back as he picked up the bag and started away. He regretted the fact that there was not enough time to drop Joyce a letter before he had to report back.

He would have gone straight back to the M.S.T. lab as he had been ordered if it hadn't been for the fact that Kelly was standing in his path.

"What's the deal?" Kelly asked with real concern. "I heard them call you up to M.S.T. and wondered if you were in trouble."

"Well, if you can consider being named to the first boarding party as being in trouble, I guess I am. I can assure you it's something that I would never have volunteered for," Glass said, still trying to control the lump. He certainly could not have Kelly believing that he was anything but a strong man incapable of petty, sentimental feelings.

Kelly looked Glass straight in the face and with real conviction said, "If it was possible I'd take your place for you, but I know they wouldn't stand still for it."

"Thanks anyway, kid," Glass replied, "but there is something that you can do for me."

"You just name it," Kelly shot back.

"Well, if I remember right you're the fellow that has the hunting knife," Glass said. "Not that I think I will need it, but if I can I would like to borrow it for a while."

"You're damned right," Kelly said as he hurried over to his locker and came back with the knife and scabbard. He pushed them into his friend's hand, wishing there was more that he could do.

"Thanks a million," Glass said as he loosened his belt and slipped the knife into it, heading back toward he didn't know what. The feel of the knife strapped to his side didn't completely ease the tension, but it gave him a feeling of some control of the future.

He had his feelings pretty well under control as he entered the M.S.T. lab for the second time.

7. NEWS CENSORED

Even though the fishermen who worked out of the harbor at Craig, Alaska, were equipped with radio receivers and they made a habit of listening to newscasters at least once during each day, none were aware of what was happening a few hundred miles to the north.

A group of skippers of trolling vessels were gathered around a table in one of the town's two taverns, grumbling about the costs of operating and the gradual decline in the number of salmon that seemed to be available. Some were in port for ice for their holds in preparation for another trip out, after selling their last catch. Others needed repairs to their vessels, or merely more fuel and supplies.

This group included the present writer, who had made the trip north to photograph fishing in the far-north state and generally view conditions. He had been a guest for several days aboard one of the trollers that originally sailed out of Ketchikan, Alaska, skippered by an old friend, Nevin May.

May had returned to port, not because his hold was full of fish but to allow the writer to catch an airplane back to Ketchikan, from where he intended to continue his research work on fishing conditions in the 49th state.

"It just seems to take longer and longer to fill the hold with fish nowadays," one of the fishermen said, adding, "I can remember not too many years ago when I could take enough ice out with me to cool my entire catch, but now it seems I have to stay out so long that I have to come in before I have a full load. Just run too low on ice."

"I don't think there is a one of us that wouldn't agree that there are just not as many fish as there was in the past, and the hell of it is there seem to be so many less each year, you wonder why you even bother to go out." Even as the speaker said this, you could see the veins in his neck swell. Because the man raised his voice to make this point, others in the tavern looked around at them.

In hope of quieting the group, May commented: "Say, that's pretty neat the way you've rigged that fence around your daughter's play area on the boat." As he said it he recalled that the fencing allowed a swing and other play items out on the deck of the fishing boat, things he had never seen on a fishing boat before.

"Well, I really had to do something. She's getting too big to confine in the cabin during play time. At least this way she gets some sunshine."

"I suppose she'll be starting school pretty soon. I can't remember how old you said she was," May replied.

"She's four now, and I guess this will be her last year on the boat. Not because we want it that way, but just the way things seem to be working out. We had even made arrangements for her to go to school in Seattle while we fished down south, and then during the summer she could come back up here fishing with us, but I just don't see how I can afford trying to make a living as a fisherman much longer. I love the outdoors and the fishing, just as my wife does, but if the fish are going to become fewer and fewer, I don't see how we can make it." As the fingers of his left hand whitened in a grip, he went on, "As you know, costs sure aren't going down as far as maintaining a fishing boat these days, and the price of fish isn't climbing enough to justify the small catches that we are getting. I can assure you I'm not looking forward to finding another means of making a living, but I just can't completely ignore the handwriting on the wall." Even as he spoke, there was no question the subject had been a matter disturbing both him and his wife for some time.

The group sat silently mulling over what he had said, occasionally taking a swallow from the bottles in front of them.

One of the other skippers who called his home port Seattle, piped up with, "I have to go along with you. I don't think I can afford to make the trip up here another year if things don't improve—either the price or the amount of fish. It doesn't look likely that either one is going to change very fast."

Several members of the group from southern ports, such as Seattle and Portland, came north each spring when the salmon season started, then moved south as the season closed in the northern waters and opened off the coast of Washington and Oregon. Thus, if they had a large enough boat, they could fish into early winter before returning to their home port to prepare their boats for the next year.

"Well, at least you fellows have the southern waters where you can make a living even if you can't afford the trip up here," May shot back. "You take us Alaskans up here, we don't have big enough boats to travel south and pick up additional income fishing down there."

With that the first fisherman slammed his bottle down on the table top to draw attention, then said, "Look, that's what I'm trying to tell you. There are a hell of a lot fewer fish down there too, so it just doesn't seem to matter where you go to fish, north or south, you burn up a hell of a lot more fuel per fish now."

"I'll be damned if I know what the answer is," one of those who had been listening commented, as he looked around at the others.

Another who had remained quiet up to that point, raised up in his chair with, "Don't tell me you don't know what the answer is. You know as well as the rest of us that if the foreign fishing fleets are going to continue dragging everything but the beer bottles out of the ocean within a couple of miles of the shoreline there are bound to be fewer and fewer fish, both up here and in the south. I'm surprised that we've been able to last as long as we have."

"I know all that crap, but what in the hell can we do about it?" another commented.

"I could give you that old s--- about writing to your congressman, but I realize that there have been a bunch of fishermen who have already done that for all the good that it has done," May explained. He went on, "If there was just some way we could get the people besides fishermen excited about it, it might help. I don't mean people in Oregon, Washington and Alaska, because I think they are already on our side. I mean those people who live in other than coastal states such as Iowa, Nebraska, and the like. Nobody writes to their congressman, and as a result nothing has ever been done to excite them."

"Well, when they see how few salmon there are in their fish market maybe they will get the message," was the answer.

"Look, most of those people never have a chance to taste salmon now, and if we wait for that to happen we may just as well forget the whole thing. They'll do without," May said.

"I have to agree with May," remarked one of the Seattle fishermen. "It goes right back to the same old story, a lot of people

in this country have a problem as far as the foreign fishing
vessels are concerned, but they prefer to hide their heads in the
sand, figuring that it isn't their problem, just ours."

"Bitching about it isn't going to get anything done. Does anyone have a suggestion as to what *can* be done about it?" came
from a Craig man.

"I know a newspaper editor from Oregon that might have a
suggestion on what to do," May said as he turned to the writer,
expecting some real gems of wisdom.

"Wait a minute fella, I can appreciate your problem but I'm
supposed to be on vacation and just taking a bunch of movies on
how you people get the job done," I glanced around at their
faces to see what the reception was going to be.

"Hell, May, you didn't tell us he was a newspaper guy. You
just told us a friend was coming up to put us in the movies."

"Well, I didn't want you fellows to think I was trying to lord
it over you because I knew some influential people," May
replied with a chuckle, then added, "I worked for him years ago
back in Oregon before coming up here."

"Well, regardless of why he came up here, I would like to
hear his answer to our problem. Seriously, I know damned well
we're going to have to have a lot of influential people on our
side if we're going to whip this thing," one of the Seattle fishermen said.

"I suppose I could get off the hook easy by just telling you
that your best bet is to hire a big national advertising company
to run a huge campaign. That would be the easiest way to
handle it if there was money galore, but without money things
are a little different." Before I could go any further, one of the
others spoke up.

"How in the hell could we provide money for an advertising
campaign when we are already pleading poverty?"

"I know what you mean," I interrupted, "because before you
could even start the advertising campaign you would have to get
some research group to come in, make a survey of how much
the foreign fishing fleets are getting, check if the building of
new dams has stopped enough salmon from reaching their
spawning grounds to bring this major change about, or if it is a
combination."

"We've all been told that with the addition of more fish
hatcheries in the states there are more salmon fingerlings nowadays than there ever were before, so you should be able to rule
out that 'dam construction' part."

"Well, now you say you heard that," I cut in, "but do you know that to be fact? You can't just go on hearsay, because as sure as hell there are going to be people that are going to be checking the matter out, and if you are wrong they are going to be throwing those facts back in your face. I'm not saying you are wrong, but unless you can back up your story with some facts you wouldn't get very far with that."

Everyone in the group leaned forward as though they were seriously interested in the discussion now. After an interruption from the bartender bringing another round of beer, May said, "What do you think is the best method of getting all the facts needed?"

I looked around at him, "Hell, Nevin, you know the answer to that as well as I do. It is either going to give a few guys a lot of work to do—or, if you can interest some other group or groups to band together with you, it would be easier. What about the packing plants? Has anyone ever asked them what they plan to do about the problem?"

From the other side of the table one of the men was quick to answer, "I talked with the plant manager over at Ketchikan a few weeks ago about it. His answer was that most of the packing plants process other foods, and if the fish industry goes to pieces they will just close the plant up, or convert to some other product. They don't seem to be getting too worked up about whether they can salmon, or something else just so they can make a profit for their stockholders."

"How about the sports fishermen? They have some pretty powerful groups going now down south," I commented, adding, "You know if you could interest them they could be a very powerful ally?"

"S---, most of them think we are the bad guys that are taking all the fish out of the ocean," someone piped up. "I doubt very much that we will ever be able to get them over to our side."

"Damn it, if you don't try you never will really know whether they would be sympathetic to your cause or not," I countered. "I could get the word out down my way, but until you got a bunch of the big groups together, you're just not going to get very far. There is always the chance that with the sports fishing groups, combined with some help from the packing plant owners, the foreign fishing limits could be moved out to at least 50 miles. I know it would be nice if it was out there 200 miles like it is off some South American countries, but 50 miles would be a hell of a help."

"It just looks to me to be one of those cases where it's too big for us and we don't seem to be able to get ourselves organized, let alone trying to get someone else organized enough to see our problem," one commented with rejection in his voice.

"I'm inclined to agree with you, and in spite of the fact that I love fishing and the outdoors, I love to eat too, and as far as I'm concerned the first guy that comes along with enough money to buy my boat I'm going to bunch it," came from across the table.

"I have to agree with you up to a point," I commented, "but you have to remember that anything that is worth having is worth fighting for. Right now I don't know what, if anything, I can do to help the cause. On top of what we have discussed, if we were ever able to get the limits moved out, we would have to turn around and help the Coast Guard get enough money to enforce the limit. They don't seem to have enough money to take care of the three-mile limit along with the other chores they have."

"I couldn't agree with you more. They do have a lot of chores, and not enough equipment to handle it. It just happens to be a good thing we fishermen stick together because when one of us gets into trouble out there, we have to depend on each other. There is just too much territory up here for the Coast Guard to give us much help. You know if something happens up here you just don't stay alive in the water very long waiting for a Coast Guard boat or plane to come a couple hundred miles looking for you."

"Yes," May said, "I'm sorry that I had my radio off at that time. We were talking and, wouldn't you know it, that was when the trouble developed. I noticed you fellows tied together off in the distance but figured you were just having a party because the fishing was so lousy about that time. I sure never dreamed that anyone was having trouble."

"We could have used a little more help in the towing, but with your radio off there was just no way we could contact you. You were headed in the opposite direction, and we knew that we were going to have to get him to a dry dock as fast as we could or we were going to lose his boat."

"Just another good reason to get out of this rat race," someone said.

"Oh, I don't mind that part of the business. It's that when something like that happens it costs and arm and a leg to get it fixed and takes several days right out of the heart of the season —and heaven only knows, we need every day of fishing that we can get to make ends meet."

"By the way," someone else chimed in, "how did the picture-taking go? Have you got some good movies of Craig's big fishing fleet?" As he asked, he leaned my way with a big smile.

"Yes, I think I have some pretty good pictures," I answered. "The only thing is you have to admit I had some stinking weather for taking pictures. I don't remember very much of the time that it wasn't drizzling or flat out raining."

"Hell, you have to get used to that if you're going to spend much time up here."

8. THE GAP CLOSES

Feeling was running high on the bridge when Captain Forsterer returned. According to the infrequent aircraft reports, one
of the fishing boats should be appearing on their radar scope.
While the rest of the officers seemed quite pleased, the captain
wondered if in fact the aircraft knew the true position of his
vessel in relation to the fishermen. No one on the *Wachusett* had
heard planes overhead, of that he was sure. He had asked the
lookouts on both bridge wings and they had given him a negative answer. Engine and other equipment noises in the pilothouse would make it difficult for anyone inside to have heard
them, but the lookouts should not have that problem. There
was always the possibility the aircraft had mistaken one of the
fishing boats for the cutter and would then believe they should
be in radar range. He could well understand how it could be
possible with the fog becoming heavier by the minute, and the
aircraft unable to just hover over an objective.

He continued to be gnawed by the fact that if the aircraft
were to lose contact with the fishermen it could be days before
they would be relocated. It would be only a miracle if the cutter
were to encounter one or more without the aid of a clear aerial
search. All he could do was continue to keep his fingers crossed
and believe that the aircraft did know the position of the
Wachusett in relation to the fishermen.

Captain Forsterer caught himself shifting from one foot to another as he waited for the radar scope to pick up one of the fishing vessels. They knew they must be close, judging from reports from aircraft hovering overhead.

As the captain tried to quiet his nerves a little, a smile crossed his face. He was thinking of Gunner's Mate First Class Paul Johnson. The information had been passed the night before that if they did overtake one of the fishing boats during the night the *Wachusett* would fire illumination shells over their head. Johnson had been so eager to fire the shells he had stayed up through the night and Captain Forsterer had been contacted numerous times during the night by the gunner's mate seeking encouragement that they might be getting closer to their objective. The captain doubted very much if the gunner's mate got any sleep at all, hoping for the chance to shoot. Probably didn't hit the sack until daylight broke, he thought, and had to smile again. Johnson had been assigned to the ship a short time before. He had been sent aboard to be Moose's replacement, but Moose hadn't been reassigned as yet, so both men were on hand for the cruise.

"They believe they have one on the fringe of our scope now, but they can't be too sure for a while."

Even as the information reached his ears, the captain was apprehensive but said, "Keep me posted. I want to know as soon as they can determine their speed and approximately how long it will be before we can overtake them."

"Captain, radar says they have a position fix now. The pip is traveling at approximately eight to ten knots and is about 15 miles away. At our present speed and course we should intercept in about an hour and a half," said Lt. jg Jones, following out the orders given earlier.

"Fine, let's get the gunners and the signalmen into position; we may be needing them sooner. If that fisherman has us on his radar he must know by now that he can't outrun us and he might just decide to stop and wait for us."

"He doesn't seem to want to wait; he is taking evasive action now."

"That makes it more interesting," the captain said as he directed Lt. Jones to keep the helmsman posted on an interception course each time the fisherman changed course.

"Apparently he is seeking the heavy fog banks to head for," the captain said, observing the clouds becoming heavier and heavier as they moved on a new interception course.

"Bearing is two one two, and closing slowly," the captain heard the radar operator call. That would be too far to have visual capability so he tried to relax, for the moment.

"Range ten thousand," said the radarman.

Ten thousand yards; five miles. Visibility in this fog was—he stared at the haze ahead—five miles? Four miles?

"Range eight thousand, closing fast," said the radarman.

This could only mean that the fisherman had decided to give up his effort to get away and had stopped his engines.

"Pass the word for the lookouts to keep their eyes peeled. We could come on this character sooner than we think. With visibility as poor as it is, we sure as hell don't want to run them down."

Ensign Jim Scott moved from one wing of the bridge to the other, passing on the latest order from the captain, while the captain himself stood staring out the front glass just hoping that he could catch sight of the fishermen.

"Range six thousand, and still closing fast."

"All ahead standard speed!" the captain called, and at the same moment asked for the messenger.

"Messenger! Write this. 'S-T-O-P.' Take that to the signal bridge. And tell them not to send too fast, and to keep repeating the message."

The captain knew it was in the blood of all signalmen to send messages as rapidly as they could, and it was always a source of gratification to them if they could burn up the recipient. In this case the recipient was a Japanese fishing vessel, unpracticed in reading messages, and possibly not even capable of reading English.

As he continued staring out the glass, he heard the alarm bell start ringing that signaled the five-inch gun mounted forward was turning. No doubt the gunners were checking the piece to make sure everything was O.K. As the gun swung to starboard, he noticed the sign they had placed there to warn seamen and others working on the deck that the gunners did not have visibility in the rear: "Man Killer"—so, beware when it was maneuvering! The alarm bell was an additional warning, but there were times in heavy seas the bell was difficult to hear. Too bad the Japanese couldn't see that sign, he thought as he watched the gun swing back to port, then back to its normal straightforward position.

Two of the Coast Guard vessels playing a role in the interception of the four Japanese gillnetters were the 269-foot icebreaker *Burton Island*, above, and the 180-foot "A" class tender *Clover*. (Photos courtesy U.S. Coast Guard)

Above: The gillnetter *Jinmei Maru* under Coast Guard aerial surveillance. Coast Guard planes were forced to keep a steady surveillance of the fishing vessels even through the night until Cutter *Wachusett* could move in for an interception. Between fog banks the task was not too difficult, but in fog and at night the vessels would run without navigation lights, making the task a real problem. Below: The gillnetter crew members stowing net on fantail. Tarp over stern obscures ship name. The stack symbol is also obscured. (Photos courtesy National Marine Fisheries Service, Dept. of Commerce)

He moved back from the glass, just as Lt. jg Jones was announcing that radar had the fishing boat within five thousand yards. He walked over to pick up his binoculars on a shelf at the back of the pilothouse, then without a word he moved to the port wing.

He knew why he had moved to that side. He wanted to make sure that everything was ready with the motor surf boat that would be launched from port. Besides, it would give him an opportunity to check the signalmen to make sure they were in their assigned position for the encounter.

One glance down told him that things must have been moving forward because the boat was not only ready, but the first boarding crew were by the rail, also at the ready. They had their life jackets strapped and apparently they had been waiting, or they were nervous, from the way they were moving about engaged in small talk.

The rattle of the lamp shutters above him indicated signalmen were already sending out the message, even though the fishermen were still not in sight.

"Boat off port bow!" someone shouted. He didn't know who, as he was too busy adjusting his glasses, but it was apparently one of the lookouts. As soon as he saw the boat, he was sure they had cut their engines and it was well that they had because with the *Wachusett's* present course they would be passing across the fishermen's bow.

"All stop!" he shouted into the pilothouse, then turned back to watch operations at the whaleboat. Everything seemed to be moving with no hitches as the boat dropped into the water and the crew hurried aboard.

Well, so much for that, he thought as he watched the boat move out in the direction of the Japanese.

He heard the click-click-click of the signal lamp while moving back toward the interior of the pilothouse. Apparently the signalmen were still trying to tell the Japanese "We're here," he figured.

"Better pass the word for the signalmen to secure," the captain said as he surveyed the officers and men on the bridge. They all seemed just to be awaiting orders.

Looking out the front glass, he noticed the five-incher was pointing directly at the fishing boat. If the Japanese were looking that way, they should get the idea we mean business, he thought as he turned back to the officers and men on the bridge.

"Keep a good eye on that boarding crew. Let me know if you see any resistance." As he passed the order he moved back onto the port wing, adjusting his glasses as he went.

"Keep that walkie-talkie open for some word," he ordered even as he was gluing his attention on the whaleboat. He knew that the boarding crew had another walkie-talkie and had been instructed to keep the *Wachusett* informed as things progressed.

9. BRIEFING

"Why in the world was I picked for this job?" Lieutenant Commander Pearson asked himself as he faced the eight men who made up the boarding parties that would attempt to secure the first two Japanese fishing vessels.

At the moment he couldn't recall why these particular men had been picked for the task. Oh, sure, there was no question that they carried ratings that could best be spared without jeopardizing the effectiveness of the ship's operation, but there were others who could have filled that category. There must have been a reason, but he certainly couldn't think what it might be.

Pearson had always been a mild-mannered fellow. One of the reasons he had entered the Coast Guard service was that it seemed there would be little or no violence connected with it, in contrast to that of the Army or Navy. After all, his family had been military people since as far back as he cared to remember. The thought now that he was going to have to instruct others into possible violence, if it became necessary, was revolting.

The captain was far better equipped mentally now to handle a situation of this kind, Pearson reasoned. After all, the duties on the bridge were not all that compelling.

His thoughts snapped back to reality as he noticed that several of the enlisted men were wearing knives on their belts as they entered the Oceanographic Lab where the briefing was to take place.

Before realizing what he was doing he blurted out, "What are the knives for, fellows?"

Fred Glass was quick to answer as he fingered the buck knife he had in a case on his belt. "There haven't been any guns or ammunition issued for this expedition and we don't have the vaguest idea what we will be running into when we get there." Glass didn't really know why he had piped up as the spokesman for the group, but he did know that he intended to have some type of protection with him on the trip.

The rest of the prize crew members voiced agreement and nodded that they were in complete accord.

The odds seemed to be against his expecting the boarding crews to go on the vessels with their hands out as though they were assigned to a welcome wagon. He excused himself and walked over to the intercom. After a brief exchange with the bridge he replaced the piece then turned back to the crews.

Another look around at the grim faces and he passed the order that they would all be allowed to carry .45's but they were only to be used in self defense. As he continued the instructions about no violence, it became obvious to him that they were no longer paying much attention. They were now busy buckling their pistols to their belts unmindful of the fact that he was still in the room. Apparently they were going to handle this assignment in their own way when they left the decks of the *Wachusett*. Following another attempt to get their attention, he just shrugged his shoulders and wished them the best of luck. He did mention that each crew would be provided with an ALPAT box that had been prepared by the Fisheries Department and included all the necessary items that would be needed while they were on the foreign vessel. He was going to go on and explain that it had been prepared by experts but he knew that he would just be talking to himself so why bother.

As the men seemed to be gathering into the two crews of four, making up those that would be together for the boarding, he was just thankful they had capable officers to accompany them. The two groups seemed to have a great deal to say to each other, all of a sudden, and they might just as well be released from the briefing as far as he was concerned.

As they filed out the door, Pearson recalled the many times before during his years with the Coast Guard that he had been forced into a position where he had what he termed a distasteful task and he didn't like it at those times any better than he did now.

The only redeeming factor to the whole mess was that just maybe the task was being forced on him so that he could again prove that he could command men. He knew in his own mind that things hadn't been the same since he had left the Supply Department, his first love. It had become apparent to him some time ago that he had been passed up when it came to issuing assignments to ships. He had always remained a junior officer regardless of where he served. As a matter of fact, this was his first crack at being an executive officer. He also had to admit to himself that this tour hadn't been what he had hoped it would be when he first came aboard.

He had reasoned at the time that he was going to be very forceful with both junior officers and enlisted men. But, after only a few days, he was finding excuses for the unmilitary behavior of the men. He just couldn't bring himself to risk losing the friendship that he felt had to be a part of his daily life. Wasn't it an old saying that you get farther with honey than you do with vinegar? Doggone it, why did it work for other people, but not for him?

After the last of the men had left the room, he glanced out and saw the surf boat had already been taken out of its blocks and was swinging over the side of the ship. It was very apparent to him that while he might dislike the idea of boarding another ship with loaded guns, the balance of the crew of the *Wachusett* were looking forward to it. And, if they weren't, they sure as shooting were putting up a good front, far better one than he felt he could under the circumstances. Right then he decided that command of a ship of his own was just not what he really wanted at all. He would take the next desk assignment that was offered, and be more than glad that he would not have to go through an ordeal such as this again.

He moved out onto the deck trying his best to avoid the hustling men who were loading supplies aboard the boat. Even though there was no fishing vessel in sight at the moment the radarman had passed the word that one of the boats was within a mile of the *Wachusett* and the distance between the two was closing fast. With the fog as heavy as it was he knew that it was unlikely that the other ship would be visible before the two were within 500 feet of each other.

Pearson leaned against the bulkhead nearby watching as the ALPAT boxes were put aboard the whaleboat. He just hoped that they really did include all the items that would be needed by the men if they were forced to stay on the fishing vessels for any length of time. He discarded the concern immediately, remembering that the Fisheries people had indicated they were experts on this type of thing and knew of all the needs that might arise. Of course, the need would only depend on whether or not it could be proved that the Japanese had been catching fish while they were east of the fisheries treaty abstention line. The Coast Guard aircraft had told them they were certain the Japanese had nets out so now it was for them to determine if the Japanese had fish in the holds of their ships. They could have disposed of the evidence, had they wanted to during the long chase, after all, it had been about 20 hours that they had been in hot pursuit of the illegal fishermen.

"Why," he thought, "had the Japanese been so unthinking as to fish that many miles inside the treaty line, and why had they refused to obey the orders when they were told to proceed to Kodiak?"

During the many hours they had been sailing full speed in pursuit of the fishing fleet radio messages had kept the *Wachusett* well appraised of what was happening. The officers had discussed the situation at some length on the bridge. They knew that the fleet had originally been discovered by a C-130 while on routine patrol, and that it had even moved down to within 50 feet of the white caps to make sure of the nationality as well as determining beyond doubt that they were in fact fishing and not just passing through the area. According to the reports, canisters had even been dropped near the fishing boats explaining in both English and Japanese that they were in illegal waters and should proceed to Kodiak. The crew members had been seen picking the canisters up from the water and, apparently reading the messages, but ignoring the instructions.

A long-range helicopter had been dispatched to the scene with a Japanese interpreter. He had tried to talk the fishermen into giving up and reversing their course. But again it was to no avail. The latest move, according to one radio message had been to load an armed crew aboard one of the new type H-3 helicopters in hopes that they could move in close enough that a boarding could be executed. The seas as high as they were with the fishing boats rising and falling as much as eight feet with the swells made the boarding move too dangerous to undertake. He had agreed with the other officers on the bridge of the *Wachusett* that such an undertaking would have been foolhardy under the very best of conditions. He just couldn't see why the

Japanese insisted upon putting up so much resistance and he continued to speculate on just how much resistance they were going to put up when the boarding party reached their vessel. He shuddered at the thought that some members of the *Wachusett's* crew might be injured or even killed before the operation was completed. Transferring men from one ship to another in normal conditions was bad enough, but now with rough water and possible resistance, the task seemed almost impossible.

"Yes," he told himself, "he would be really glad when this assignment was completed, not just this encounter, but when the entire cruise was over."

He started to move away realizing that he was contributing nothing to the activity going on around him, theorizing that if he were to move back to the bridge and trouble should develop he might be expected to issue orders that could well conflict with his feelings. So he moved a bit farther from the immediate area and continued to watch the activities.

He noticed, now that the loading had been completed and the boarding crew had little to do but wait for the whaleboat to be lowered into the water, things were changing. While they had appeared to be an almost jolly bunch at the beginning, now they didn't appear to have a great deal to say to each other. It must be that they were beginning to realize how serious their mission was. He had figured it was serious from the very start but had wondered if he was the only one that shared that feeling.

With the exception of an occasional bitch about how those Mae West life jackets were cutting off circulation, the boarding crew stood silent. He had to agree with them about the life jackets, they were awfully uncomfortable to wear for any length of time, but they were still a good deal better for this type of operation than the big bulky ones.

He felt a chill as the wind and mist continued to envelop everyone on the deck. He hadn't taken the time to put on heavier clothes because he had only figured on talking with the boarding parties and then returning to the bridge where it was reasonably warm. Now while waiting to get close enough to the fishing boat, he was feeling the effect of the weather.

Although the wait was only a bit over half an hour it had seemed more like a couple of hours. Not just to himself but he was sure the crew members felt the same way. At last Boatswain's Mate Hughes moved to the controls of the whaleboat waiting until it hit the water before starting the engine. His crew, in the boat with him, was eagerly awaiting the time when they would be able to bring the boarding crew into the whale-boat with them. The prize crew themselves appeared ready to vault over the rail and take their places, but the whaleboat still hadn't touched the water.

Things started moving fast when the whaleboat did touch the water. The *Wachusett* hadn't come to a complete stop yet but the lines kept the whaleboat moving right along with the cutter. The crew started assisting the boarding party not only to the boat but also to a seat to maintain a reasonable balance.

Pearson quickly looked around expecting to see the Japanese boat but from his vantage point was unable to do so. By moving into the wind slightly and straining his eyes he was just able to make out the shape of a fishing boat off the port quarter through the fog. As he watched the chattering boat crew fell silent and the only noise to indicate that a boat was even there was the engine as it purred, awaiting a signal from Lt. Strace-ner to go. Then with a push on the boat hooks by the crew, the whaleboat was on its way. He shivered again as he thought of the task that lay ahead of them.

As they began to disappear in the mist and fog, he wondered why he should be reminded that their wake headed straight for the fishing boat should look so much like that of a torpedo.

It was with that thought in mind that he wished for two things. The first being that there would be no evidence aboard the fishing vessel allowing the boarding crew to merely make an inspection without any chance of violence and be able to return to the *Wachusett* unharmed. The second that this infernal weather would clear up. After all with good weather the crew could bask, maybe fish a little, or whatever. Anyway you looked at it they were a happier bunch in good weather, and that made less problems for the executive officer on any ship.

The four men who would make up the second boarding party stood along the rail watching every rise and fall of the boat. Lt. Commander Pearson knew that they were well aware of the fact that if trouble was going to develop it would most likely happen to the first boarding crew.

"Do you think they'll have any problem?" one of them asked, knuckles whitening from the grasp he had on the ship's rail.

"How in hell would we know," was the answer, as though speaking for the other three, "just keep your eyes on them and you'll find out as soon as we do." There was plenty of sarcasm in his voice.

The waiting seemed to be taking its toll of them all as they followed the journey of the whaleboat.

The 255-foot U.S. Coast Guard Cutter *Wachusett* as it appeared to Japanese fishermen before boarding crews were sent aboard. The cutter intercepted two of the poaching gill-netters, providing boarding crews, and escorted the four invaders to Kodiak, Alaska, where they were detained. Below: The U.S. Coast Guard Cutter *Wachusett*'s motor surfboat provided the transportation to the Japanese gillnetter for the boarding parties. (Photos courtesy Lt. Cmdr. Robert H. Stracener, U.S. Coast Guard)

Above: Japanese gillnetter *Kamome Maru 20* was one of four boarded by the Coast Guard off Alaska coast. From the extra fuel barrels along the aft rail, she was intending a long trip. Below: A closeup of the *Jinmei Maru* pilothouse, center of operations with an excellent view of nets coming aboard. (Photos courtesy National Marine Fisheries Service, Dept. of Commerce, and Lt. Cmdr. Robert H. Stracener, U.S. Coast Guard)

"You know I was fairly proud that I was picked for this job in the beginning, but now I'm not so damned sure I even want to go through with it," drifted up to Lt. Cmdr. Pearson.

"Oh, just cool it. Everything's going to be all right," someone answered.

"I honestly wish I was with them," Kelly said in passing, "at least they will be where the action is, if there is any. We are going to have to just stand here for God only knows how long waiting for our turn. I'll tell you another thing, I'm sure glad we were able to talk the brass into letting us have sidearms. I feel one hell of a lot better with that thing at my side."

"Oh crap, if something was to happen some Japanese will probably shove that gun right down your throat," another comment by the Coastie displaying the sarcasm to hide the concern he was experiencing.

10. TAKING OVER

The five men had very little to say to each other as they climbed into the diesel-powered whaleboat for the start of the trip to the Japanese ship. While the waves had not seemed that large aboard the *Wachusett*, they became very ominous as the small boat slipped up and down the cutter's hull, some six to eight feet with each swell, before a push or two on boat hooks got them started on their way.

The Fisheries Officer, Craig Hammond, continued to remain to himself, as he had throughout the cruise, as far as enlisted men were concerned. This was Hammond's first boarding for the purpose of seizing a vessel. He had been on numerous courtesy boardings where they checked the catch and gear used by a foreign vessel, but this trip was for real. He had spent four years in the Coast Guard, even rising to the rank of lieutenant before joining the National Marine Fisheries Service, but there was a real sense of anticipation now. The other four members of the crew were more concerned about their own well-being than they were about him at the point in time.

They wondered if they had dressed warmly enough as the cold wind sent shivers through their bodies. Glass, who was still not sure why he had been picked for the assignment, began to wonder if it was the weather alone that was causing the chills. He could think of a great many places he would rather be than in a boat headed for heaven-only-knew what.

As the *Wachusett* grew smaller in their wake, and the fishing boat appeared much larger than it had before, the cold spray from the top of an occasional wave made the entire scene even more menacing. None of them were the least bit sure what the reception was going to be when they reached the fishermen. They only knew that there were several of them lined along the rail and each time their craft reached the top of a swell, and the visibility was better, it became obvious that some of the fishermen were waving fists and chattering in Japanese, which none of them could understand.

The trip across, while taking only a matter of minutes, seemed to stretch into hours—but now that they were drawing closer and the bobbing in the whaleboat was not all that much fun, they were still not sure that they wanted the trip to come to an end. They had received their orders and under the circumstances they knew there was no turning back, regardless of what the reception would be.

Glass had carried a .45 automatic on numerous occasions during his years in the service, and many times had carried live ammunition, but the gun felt much heavier at his side now than it ever had before, and he found that his hand would continually drop to his side to raise the holster to relieve the weight from his hip. He knew that he shouldn't take it from its holster before climbing aboard the ship, because he would no doubt need both hands for the task of getting to the deck. He also knew well that a person could survive only about six minutes in that water, and he certainly didn't want to have to rely on the Japanese crew to pull him from the ocean. The members of the whaleboat crew were dressed in wet suits, and they would make every effort to rescue anyone who fell in, but that was little consolation when you knew that the whaleboat would be maneuvering dangerously close to the fishing boat for such an operation. No, that just didn't sound like too much fun.

"When we get aboard, Glass, you take over the bridge. Franklin, you check below decks with the Fisheries Officer, and Dempsey and I will secure things on the main deck," Lieutenant Stracener said half-heartedly. Glass looked over at him to see if he issued the orders only to establish confidence in the other three, or if it was just to bolster his own feelings. There was no doubt now that the lieutenant was as nervous, if not more so, than the other three in the boarding crew.

Glass wondered about the orders at the time; it just seemed logical that the lieutenant, being the senior officer in this boarding party, would want to be the person who encountered the captain of the ship. However, it had been pointed out to them that the securing of the evidence that the Japanese had been illegally fishing was also very important. Possibly the lieutenant figured that he could direct operations better from the main deck. Glass thought of the old saying, "Theirs not to reason why. Theirs but to do and die." Right at that point the words didn't seem to have the humor connected with them that they normally had.

His mind moved to other things as he saw the orange hull of the fishing boat coming closer; thoughts of the whaleboat being slammed against the side came to mind. Gad! I would hate like hell to be to be tossed into the water here, he said to himself as he visioned the boat flipping as it moved up and down the orange hull. Even though they hadn't reached the ship yet, he wondered just how much help or hindrance those men lining the rail were going to offer when they did reach the side.

Boatswain's Mate Hughes, who was operating the surfboat, explained to the men that he was going to pull as close to the fishing craft as possible, and it would then be up to them to get aboard as best they could. No one questioned this. They all knew that to have the whaleboat remain close to the fishing boat would be inviting trouble. With waves as high as they were running, the whaleboat could easily be crushed against the heavier hull of the fishing boat, and they could all wind up in the freezing-cold water of the Pacific.

The fishing craft was riding quite low in the water and if they played their cards right they could almost step aboard when they reached the crest of a wave—that is if the distance between the two was not too great at the time. In spite of the fact that the crucial moment was yet to come, Glass unbuckled a couple of the fasteners of his life jacket. He didn't want to have it hindering his maneuvering when and if he reached the deck.

Hughes proved again his superior ability to handle a small boat. It had long been known on the *Wachusett* that he could handle a boat nearly as well as he could play poker. The boat smoothly moved into a wave, seeming to ride with it along the side of the Japanese vessel and make the boarding appear an almost simple affair. The chance of being dashed to pieces by the force of the sea was unthought of as they slowly grazed the bigger boat's side. Everything happened so fast no one appeared to give it any serious thought.

As Glass mounted the steps to the pilothouse of the fishing vessel, several thoughts went through his mind. He vaguely recalled, as he was slipping through the rail, that the fishermen who had been lined along the side had indicated that they had no intention of being the least bit cooperative to those in the boarding party. They hadn't offered any resistance to the boarding, and in his haste he had merely dodged a couple of them, discarding his life jacket in the process. He recalled that he had even tossed the life jacket back into the whaleboat.

Now that he was bounding up the ladder to the bridge, he wondered what the reception was going to be once he reached his objective. As he approached the door of the pilothouse he realized for the first time that he had his .45 in his right hand. He couldn't for the life of him remember taking the weapon from its holster. He did remember thinking about the gun while he was still in the whaleboat, and at the time realized that it could well be a detriment if he were to draw it before actually boarding the fishing boat. At that point, who was to know if even two hands would be enough to keep one from being dumped into the sea?

His eyes took in the full scope of the pilothouse interior as the door opened to his push. From the earphones it was obvious that one of the three men he encountered was the radio operator. He thought how funny the earphones looked on him because of the flatness of his head. He was about five-foot-seven with glasses. He seemed to be well groomed and had fairly long hair. The second man did not wear a uniform, but it was apparent that he must be the captain when he bowed again and again as Glass entered. He seemed to be just slightly taller than the radio operator but he had short hair and didn't wear glasses.

The third man, who appeared very well dressed, was about the same height as the radio operator. He didn't wear glasses either but did look a little out of place being so well dressed on a fishing boat. He had piercing eyes that gave Glass the feeling that the man was looking straight through him. The fact that he stood apart from the other two had Glass wondering for the moment. Nevertheless, he knew that it was his job to take over the bridge and that was just what he meant to do as he shoved the .45 automatic forward for all three to see. If he received any greeting it was all silence, but at least it wasn't menacing as he believed it might be.

The radio operator stood with his mouth ajar, the blank look on his face translating the thought he must have had—he just didn't believe it could happen. The captain was still bowing but was now chattering as he came up from each bow. Glass didn't have the slightest idea what he was saying but he did notice that there was a broad smile on his face, so assumed it must be something pleasant. The third man, still standing apart from the others, was glaring not only at Glass but also the others, apparently not in the least bit happy with the turn of events.

Glass wondered if he should have had the three put their hands in the air while he had them at gunpoint, but now that he had been with them for several minutes he really didn't see any reason for it. He wondered how he would have signaled them to put their hands up, even if he had thought of it at the time he first entered the pilothouse. Oh, well, what did it matter—the three seemed to be keeping their place now.

As he continued to eye them he noticed they were not really concentrating on either him or the .45 he still held in his hand. They were looking out the window behind him. Thinking it might be a trick to get him to look around, he ignored the matter for a few more minutes, but then the urge became too great. He looked over his shoulder and could see why they seemed so engrossed in the view. The *Wachusett* had either drifted or been maneuvered much closer to the fishing craft. At the moment it looked huge, riding the waves a few yards from the fishing boat, but the thing that had grown out of all proportion was the five-inch gun. He knew it was only a five-inch gun, but with the barrel pointed directly at the pilothouse it appeared to be bigger than any cannon he had ever seen before. He was sure the gun had the same effect on the three men he was with. Under the circumstances he could see no more need to hold the gun pointed at them. He was convinced they weren't about to play any games with him, at least not for the present.

He slipped the gun back into its holster but didn't snap the catch closed, just in case he found a need to get back to it.

Unconsciously he reached into his pocket and pulled out a cigarette. Long before he could fish a match from his pocket, the captain was holding a flame for him. While he didn't think the act was all that odd, apparently the well-dressed man in the group did. He snapped out a few words of Japanese and the captain jumped back. Not only did he jump back from Glass, but he also wiped the silly grin he had been wearing from his face. Now there was little question in Glass's mind as to who was the big wheel on the bridge of this vessel. He hadn't really cared for the man's appearance when he first entered the pilothouse but thought much less of him now. For a moment he was tempted to bring the gun back out and point it at the one man only, but dropped the thought as he heard commotion on the deck below.

A quick look below relieved his mind. It appeared that Lt. Stracener was calling the two Coasties and the Fisheries Official together for a conference. Glass knew that they would pass the word to him as soon as something had been decided.

11. RESISTANCE?

Watching Fred Glass take over the bridge of his ship with a .45 automatic poised in his hand had the skipper of the Japanese fishing boat reviewing in his mind the whole operation. Why in hell did he ever listen to Yokoma in the first place, he asked himself. Then as though answering himself he reasoned: Yes, it had all started early in the season when the four boats had left Japan. Yokoma had been assigned to them as the fishing manager, therefore it was his decision as to where they would fish and for how long.

They had been lucky the first three times out. Each trip they moved closer to the abstention line in order to fill the ship's hold. But this trip out, things were not going all that great until they moved into illegal waters. He had cautioned the fish manager about the advisability and had discussed the matter with the other captains. They had agreed with him that they didn't think it was a good idea, but inasmuch as there was only one fish manager they were supposed to take their orders from him. They could have radioed the home office and possibly had his orders countermanded, but they felt it would not be good business putting information such as that out on the air waves. Thus here they were now in serious trouble.

Yokoma knew very well that the treaty between the United States, Canada and Japan meant that they were not to fish inside 175 degrees west longitude, but he also knew that as the season progressed fish were harder to come by unless the ships fudged a little. He had been successful in evading detection in the past and was sure that his luck would hold out again this time. He always made sure that his ships only slipped into illegal water during bad weather, thus avoiding the patrol planes and ships.

As far as the Coast Guard cutters were concerned, they could usually listen to reports from other fishermen and know their location at all times. He had realized that he was gambling a little heavier this trip but at the rate they were pulling fish in, it wasn't going to take them long to get a load and head for home.

The skipper told himself again that he and the other captains could have put up a fuss and very likely have overruled the fish manager when he first suggested crossing the line, but the idea didn't seem so bad at the time. Now as he eyed the gun in the young Coast Guardsman's hand he continued to bow as though he didn't have the vaguest idea of what in the world this was all about, and just what they expected from him.

He recalled that when they had first come across the invisible line, fishing had been very spotty, and it seemed the farther they moved into illegal waters the better the fishing became. With the almost continuous fog it just didn't seem possible they would be detected.

Yokoma had told them that all information he had picked up indicated there was only one buoy tender and one cutter trying to patrol the entire area. The cutter had been last seen patrolling in the Bering Sea and the buoy tender was so slow they wouldn't have any trouble outrunning it if they were seen. So, under the circumstances, it seemed they could get their load of fish and be on their way without anyone being the wiser. Anyway, he knew of many other Japanese fishing fleets that had got away with it, so it was a calculated risk that they could. He still believed that if they had not developed engine trouble they still could have succeeded. Weren't they the only ones who had been caught? He didn't have any idea whether the cutter would be able to catch any of the other fleet members. The cutter didn't appear to have caught up with them very fast, but he had no way of knowing how fast it really was. They had been so busy seeking out fog banks and altering their course he was sure they had lost ground in their run.

That damned Coast Guardsman isn't to be kidded, the skipper mused as he noticed the determined look on the other's face and the menacing way he waved that gun. There was little doubt that the young man wanted them just to stay put for the time being. They didn't dare play any more games with him after noticing the strain on his trigger finger, nor did he have any intention of giving his life for a few tons of fish.

As the captain stopped his bowing and moved to the back of the pilothouse waiting for the Guardsman's next move, he wondered if they should stick to their story about the faulty navigational aids or the one they had talked over about not knowing anything about any nets. He could see that the crew was being kept under control for the moment at gunpoint by other Guardsmen on deck. He hadn't really paid any attention to just how many of them had been in the boarding party, but apparently there had been more than he had thought. From the look of things there must still be several of them below decks—how many he had no idea.

He turned and looked down at his crew who were in turn giving most of their attention to him, as though just waiting for him to give them some orders. He felt a little sorry for the poor devils; they realized little or nothing of what was going on. They would have had no way of knowing that the entire fleet had been fishing in forbidden territory. Only he, the radioman and Yokoma were aware of exactly where they had been. Even if the crew had been told, he was sure that their desire to get a quick load of fish and get out would have been their choice too. That still didn't alter the fact that at present they had no idea why these Coast Guardsmen were aboard their ship, but he felt for the time being maybe he had best let them think what they would. There was time enough to tell them if it later became necessary.

As he watched affairs on the main deck, he realized that because the crew members did not have any inkling of the violation, they appeared to be a bit irritated by the Coast Guardsmen's intrusion. Watching them, he began to be afraid that there might be trouble. They were starting to mill around the two guardsmen on the deck, in a hostile manner, so he decided that he was going to have to quiet them. While he still had no intention of disclosing the real reason for the guardsmen boarding, he did lean out a pilothouse window to pass the word for them to be hospitable to the Americans.

Glass had previously wondered if he should have had the three put their hands in the air while he had them at gunpoint, but now that it appeared the captain had made the move to quiet the crew, he didn't feel the need. He now began to wonder how he would have signaled them to put their hands up, even if he had thought of it at the time he first entered the pilothouse. In any case, it presently looked as if things were completely under control on the deck, so why worry.

As long as the three Japanese were on the far side of the pilot-house and making no hostile moves, Glass took enough time to glance down at the deck. It was apparent that after the word passed through the ranks of the crew there was a difference in their attitude toward his shipmates. While they still did not look upon the Americans as friends, at least it didn't appear that they were ready to throw the intruders off their ship.

The captain, however, sensed that he would only have to give the word and the situation could have been one of all-out war, and there was little doubt that someone would have been hurt.

He thought, half in amusement, that they could have assumed it was nothing other than the high-and-mighty U.S.A. sending armed ships into the Pacific just to harass Japanese fishermen as they attempted to eke out a meager living from the international waters. Yes, he could see why the crew would be irritated, and he was going to remember their willingness to defend both him and the ship regardless of the odds.

There hadn't been any doubt in his mind before that he had a good and loyal crew, but now his feeling for them was much more endearing. They had done a great deal of fishing together in the past and when this mess was cleared up, and if the company still retained him as one of the captains, he was certainly going to do everything in his power to keep this very same crew.

Even though the captain was placing the blame for the incident mainly on Yokoma's shoulders, the third man in the pilot-house, he knew down deep that he was going to have to assume some.

Meanwhile, Yokoma continued to frown at the captain as he heard him tell the crew members that they should treat the Americans with respect. After all, why should they show any respect for them? This incident was certainly going to put them all in disrespect when they reached home. In addition to that, it was very likely that he would have to find another job if they didn't succeed in convincing the Americans that they had not been in anything but international waters. Maybe the story about navigational aids malfunctioning would work. Otherwise, there was sure to be a fine, and heaven only knew what other troubles to face. Common sense told him that the Americans might believe that one ship could have malfunctioning aids, but how do you ex-lain four vessels with the same problem? No, he just couldn't see any good coming out of this whole mess, and he couldn't see why they should be nice to the policemen who were arresting them— and that, thanks to the captain, was what was happening.

As he kicked a coil of rope he rationalized that if the damned captain had continued to run it was still likely that they could have found enough fog, and by maneuvering could have got far enough into neutral water that the Coast Guard would have given up the chase. If they had moved far enough away from the other fleet vessels, the Americans would have had an awfully hard time proving they had been among the violators. They had had the cutter on their radar screen for some time and could only figure it was their lack of speed that had made them the scapegoat rather than one of the other fishing boats.

No, he decided, as long as they were in control of this ship he could see no reason to be nice to them. Hell, his boat might have been less than 60 miles from Kodiak when they were fishing and first saw an airplane, but he didn't see how—if they had got a few more miles away—it could have been proved that it was their fishing boat and not some other one.

If he could get that radio operator and the captain to stick to the story that they didn't have any nets out, they might still pull this out of the bag. Even though he thought that might be the im-mediate answer to the problem, what about the nets? They were pretty valuable and there was little doubt if they went back to Japan without them someone was going to have to pay dearly. The company had a lot of money tied up in that fishing gear, and the fact that they had run off and abandoned it wouldn't set too well.

Sure, the company would really lay it in his lap. They would inform him that he knew that the international treaty called for their being outside the 175-degrees-west mark. He could justify it in his mind because even though Japan had signed the treaty with the United States and Canada there were a great many countries that hadn't paid any attention to the line—Korea, China and Russia, to name just a few. The whole matter just didn't make sense to him. If he had his way he would have the crew throw the Americans overboard and still make a run for it. He hoped that the other three vessels in the fleet would make good their escape and then laugh their fool heads off at this captain for getting caught.

There was only one drawback now: that gun in this Coast Guardsman's hand and that big gun on the cutter. He didn't know if either would be used, but he had better wait a little to see what happened next.

12. SECURING THE VESSEL

Glass and the three Japanese didn't have long to wait, as minutes go, before Lt. Stracener and Craig Hammond, the Fisheries Officer, made their appearance. Lt. Stracener entered the now-crowded pilothouse while Hammond stood at the door awaiting further orders. It appeared he had completed his inspection of things below decks where he had gone immediately after boarding. It was his task to check the amount and kind of fish, if any, that had been stowed by the Japanese. It was evident from the look on his face that he had uncovered enough evidence that the vessel had been poaching in U.S. waters to merit seizure.

Hammond seemed quite thrilled with the idea of seizure because this was the first time he had taken part in a major caper of this kind since going to work for the National Marine Fisheries Service. Right now there was every possibility that if they caught all four vessels in this fleet it would be the largest single action in which the Coast Guard or N.M.F.S. had ever been involved.

He and Lt. Stracener discussed the evidence for a short time before the lieutenant unlimbered the walkie-talkie he had brought with him. A short conversation with the bridge of the *Wachusett* brought the cutter up to date with what had transpired to that moment. After the cutter had been assured that things were under control aboard the fishing boat, the walkie-talkie came alive with orders for both Stracener and the Fisheries Officer.

When the instrument finally went dead, Stracener turned to Hammond, "I guess they want you back on the *Wachusett* right away," adding, "they're ordering the whaleboat to pick you up."

The whaleboat, which had been circling up to that point, straightened its course and headed toward the fishing boat. It was apparent that the whaleboat was also in walkie-talkie contact with the cutter. As Hughes brought the small boat alongside the *Jinmei Maru* for the second time, Hammond jumped aboard with two of the seamen helping to prevent his falling over the other side. Without so much as a wave they were off in the direction of the cutter.

It gave the members of the boarding party a feeling of emptiness as they watched the whaleboat disappearing into the fog toward what had been their home for some time. The *Wachusett* had maneuvered away to a safe distance from the fishing vessel, and only the silhouette of the cutter was visible as it lay-to in the distant mist.

They had only the occasional crackling of the walkie-talkie to tell them that they were not completely alone in the world filled with Japanese fishermen. They knew then that the future of the *Jinmei Maru No. 8* was in their hands and they had best make some friends in a hurry if they were to survive.

Now that things had quieted off somewhat, the five men began to realize that the ten-by-three-foot pilothouse had not been constructed to accommodate that many people. Even though things were crowded, Stracener knew he would need everyone to execute the orders he had been given just a few minutes before.

"Glass, we're going to have to figure out a way to communicate with them, because we have to get this boat moving."

"Shee-it," Glass said after glancing around at the three Japanese he and the lieutenant had been trying to converse with. "I believe we have a batch of people here that just don't know how to read." He and Stracener had been passing "Tri-Language" cards around, pointing out Japanese characters that were matched with an English counterpart. The officers would just look, then shrug their shoulders as though it were all Greek to them. There was just no question but that they were going to have to find another method to communicate with them.

"We have just got to get this boat moving!" Stracener repeated to Glass, as he looked around the bridge of the ship to see if there was an indication from the Japanese that they were comprehending in any way.

Although Stracener was a bare five-foot-ten-inches tall he seemed to tower over the Japanese as they all exchanged glances. Then turning as though pleading to Glass he said, "We just have to get this thing moving. The cutter has indicated that they are going after another of the fishing boats and we are to follow them by steering a course of 235 degrees. Right now I don't know just how in the world we are going to get the word to these guys, but we are going to have to find some way to do it, and we're going to have to do it pretty fast. The cutter wants us to try to keep up with them."

Glass looked first at the fish manager, and it was obvious from the icy stare from him there was little chance for any cooperation. He took in the captain then, who appeared to think the whole thing was one big joke, so there didn't seem to be much use trying to get anything out of him. That left the radio operator, who at the moment was standing next to Glass. He wasn't sure, but there did seem to be a slight look of compassion for them on his face. Naturally that would have to be the place to start.

"Let me take a crack at it," said Glass as he nudged the radio operator toward the compass. He merely pointed to the compass heading that they were to proceed in, and gave the man another nudge with his shoulder. Then he indicated with his hand that he wanted an invisible throttle moved forward. He reasoned that if the man had ever operated a small boat he would know what the signals meant.

The radio operator fumbled around a bit, but was trying to turn around for an indication from the other two Japanese just what they expected of him. Glass immediately stepped between them so that a signal between them would be impossible. The radioman tried several times to look back, then realized that he was pretty much on his own. Glass ventured a quick glance over his shoulder and noted that the silly grin had left the captain's face; and if looks could kill, he would certainly be dead from the scowl he was receiving from the fish manager. There was little doubt they disapproved of the radioman helping in any way.

He believed for a minute that he was going to have to add another nudge or two before the radioman was going to cooperate, but finally the fellow started pushing a button that was ringing a bell in the engine room. At that moment things were quiet enough on the bridge so that they could hear the bell, then the engines start. Glass knew he was on the right track now. He again moved forward indicating with his finger the course to be steered. Then he motioned with his invisible throttles that he wanted full speed. He thought for a moment he might have to intercede as the radioman started pushing levers that were not at first familiar, but on closer inspection he realized that they were only to engage the automatic pilot mechanism. The *Wachusett* did not have an automatic pilot, and while the submarines he had served on did, he had never made a serious inspection of them.

When the radioman completed his tinkering, he looked around again for approval from the captain, and when the captain just turned and looked the other way, he pushed the bell button again and they started forward. The vessel took off as though it were going to jump completely out of the water. Both Glass and Lt. Stracener were caught off guard and were forced to grab something to steady themselves as the boat surged ahead, like nothing they had experienced before.

When they had regained their footing, Glass moved up behind the radioman saying, "You do fine job, si, si, good." He realized as he said it that he had his languages mixed up. Then it came to him, "ga-dime-sh," or something like that, was "thank you" in Japanese. But he didn't think too much of the fellow not knowing what he was saying because the radioman had a pleased expression on his face as he looked up at Glass. "Good old Charlie," he continued as he gave the man a meaningful tap on the shoulder.

The radioman turned with the smile still on his face, "Me Charlie." The minute he said it he knew he shouldn't have because the fish manager really lit into him. It wasn't necessary to know the language to know that he was being bawled out, but it also told the Coast Guardsmen that the radio operator was not completely ignorant of the English language.

"You know we are going to have to learn what their bell signals are," Lt. Stracener said, "so they won't be able to pull anything on us in the future."

Glass turned his attention from Charlie to the lieutenant just in time to see his eyes grow wide.

"Look out!" Stracener cried. "We're going to run the *Wachusett* down." As he moved forward toward the wheel of the fishing craft, the stern of the cutter became larger and plainer through the fog. It was apparent now that they were on the same course and would be running them down if something wasn't done and done fast. The *Wachusett* was faster, but certainly did not have the capability to get underway as quickly. While it was now moving, it was not going nearly as fast as the craft they were on, and total destruction appeared to be close at hand.

Lt. Stracener's move to the wheel was a useless effort because without disengaging the automatic pilot, changing course was out of the question. Even though he tugged at the wheel several times, he failed to realize that when this automatic pilot was locked in, she was locked in, and no one was going to change the course.

Even as the *Wachusett* appeared to be impossible to miss, the radioman moved forward, disengaged the pilot, and twisted hurriedly on the wheel. As the two vessels passed it was apparent that with one more coat of paint on either there would have been some type of contact made. Faces of those watching, aboard both vessels, became chalky white as the passing took place.

"Wow, that was close," said Glass as he let his breath out slowly.

Even though he was still trying to figure out how the two ships managed to keep from colliding, he looked around at the others. With the exception of the radioman, the Japanese seemed to be paralyzed, with their eyes glued straight forward. A glance at the lieutenant showed that he wasn't yet over the shock of the near miss.

As the two vessels pulled farther and farther apart, Stracener regained control of himself and indicated to the radioman that he could engage the automatic pilot again, now that the danger was over. It was obvious from the shaking of the radioman's hand that he hadn't completely mastered his control yet, but he did as he had been signaled to do and then moved back.

A pin would have made a tremendous crash landing on the deck of the pilothouse during the next few minutes, as quiet as it was.

Things had barely returned to anything close to normal aboard the fishing boat when the captain pointed out the white shape of the cutter on the starboard side as she gained speed and was pulling past them. The walkie-talkie in Lt. Stracener's hand came alive as they watched the second passing. Everyone in the pilothouse could hear the message. They were to make every effort to keep up with the cutter, and they were not only to make sure they kept the *Wachusett* on their radar scope, but were also to maintain contact on the walkie-talkie as long as possible. The cutter was on her way to catch the second fishing vessel if possible. There was no mention of the near miss during the message transmission.

As they moved off in pursuit of the cutter, Glass began to wonder why none of the three Japanese had made any effort to signal the engine room to stop engines, when they were bearing down so fast on the cutter. He knew that the controls of the ship and the surroundings were so new to both Lt. Stracener and himself—plus the speed of activities—that they were both more or less spellbound. Even if either had wanted to do something about the engines, neither knew what the bell signals of the Japanese were.

As he thought more about it he was glad the radioman had the presence of mind to move into action. It was a cinch that the other two Japanese on the bridge were not moving in any direction to save the ship.

"Boy, now I know we want to find out what the bell signals are," Stracener said, "and I think the sooner we learn them the better."

"Maybe I can get it from my friend Charlie, here," Glass said as he turned to the radio operator and started making slow conversation. After several tries, he turned to the lieutenant, "I'm afraid that bawling out he received awhile ago has left Charlie deaf and dumb again."

"I'm inclined to agree. We will just have to get them separated, if we are going to do any good at all." With that the lieutenant looked hard at both the captain and the fish manager, hoping that they understood what he had said. If they did, they never let on because they continued to stand by scowling at not only the Coast Guardsmen but the radio operator as well.

13. ANOTHER TRY

Captain Forsterer turned and started back into the pilothouse of the *Wachusett* as soon as he saw the surfboat bobbing through the water on its way back from the *Jinmei Maru No. 8*.

"Ensign Donaldson, I want that whaleboat loaded aboard faster than it has ever been done before. I want to be underway as soon as possible, and have that Fisheries man come to the bridge as soon as he is aboard," the captain ordered as soon as he was inside the wing door.

The ensign knew as deck officer that it was his duty to oversee the task and that the orders meant right then. He lost no time heading down to where he could observe the entire operation.

Capt. Forsterer had his mind made up that he was going to catch at least one more of the fishing boats, and the only way that could be accomplished was to lose no time in getting underway again. He was sure the second fishing boat would know of the first capture; if not by radio, they would at least have got some idea from their radar scope. They would have been able to monitor the two pips coming close together and then both apparently standing idle for a time. Yes, they would be certain to know, and now they would be making a renewed effort to get away.

"Did radar get an estimated speed on that second fishing boat before we stopped?" the captain asked, not looking at anyone in particular.

"Yes," Jones replied. "They had the second boat moving at between 10 and 12 knots and they estimated they would be 20 to 25 miles away by now. The C-130 is having trouble keeping a bead on them. It seems those wooden vessels are pretty hard for them to keep track of."

"Well, if we can get going right away we should be able to get them back on our radar screen in an hour or so and then we won't need the aircraft. They can concentrate on the two that the *Burton Island* will have to intercept." After he made the comment, he realized that he was admitting to the other officers he had given up hope of the *Wachusett* catching more than two of the violators. He headed back for the wing to see how the loading of the surfboat was coming.

I'm going to have to compliment that boatswain's mate first chance I get, he told himself as he watched the smooth, fast maneuvering and loading taking place below him. That guy really knew his job.

Ensign Donaldson and Hammond were entering just as Forsterer was returning from the wing. The ensign was just beginning to say something, but he was waved to silence as the captain turned to Jones and issued orders for Stracener and his prize crew to steer on a 235-degree course and to try to stay in radar range if they could. Then he added, "And let's get this thing underway!" He had made up his mind that he was going to interpret the order to keep a ship with a boarding crew aboard in view as meaning on his radar scope. After all, in weather as mucky as this, how else could it be interpreted? With that he turned and started discussing the evidence that had been found on the *Maru No. 8.*

He was just saying, "Well, at least they didn't dispose of the evidence," when someone, he didn't know who, chimed in with "Wow!" He looked up just in time to see the fishing vessel slipping past them on the port side with barely inches to spare.

"What the hell do they think they're doing?" he asked, as he watched them pass on ahead.

The helmsman stood at the wheel in shock, then as the fishing boat angled off, making a collision less likely, he looked around as though he were expecting an order to change course. The order never came and the fishing boat started fading into the fog.

"Lt. Jones, you better have radar keep a close watch on them, they act like they have been hitting the bottle," Captain Forsterer said, having completely lost his trend of thought regarding evidence of illegal fish or fishing. "They sure must have gotten that thing going in a hurry. It's just too bad they don't know how to steer the son-of-a-bitch."

The captain was just about to renew his conversation with Hammond when Donaldson asked if it would be all right to secure the gunners and signalmen who were still at their stations. "Yes, but you had better tell them to stay on the ready. With any luck at all we'll be getting that other boat on the scope soon."

"We are going to be wanting those fishermen to go back and get their nets out of the water," Hammond was telling the captain when word came that the second vessel was now on the screen. The captain had already rationalized that the nets were going to be prime evidence in the case against the Japanese, but first he had to catch that second vessel.

It had just been pointed out by the radar, and a little calculating by Lt. Jones, that the *Wachusett* on their present course would be able to intercept in approximately three hours. This seemed to be very encouraging news to everyone on the bridge.

"Pass the word to Lt. Stracener and his crew to start working on those Japanese to get the other vessels to stop. Tell them they don't have a chance to get away, and they might just as well start working on them for the location of their nets," the captain said, turning to Lt. Jones.

"Right away, sir. He has requested their exact location at the time of boarding so he can enter it into the ship's log," Lt. Jones replied, looking to the captain for approval.

"Fine, give him the information and tell him to keep coming or we'll lose sight."

"Now where were we?" the captain asked as he turned back to Hammond. He was about to say more when the messenger handed him a message from the radio room.

"Hey, get a load of this," he said eyeing the slip of paper. "The *Burton Island* has one of the fishing boats on their radar now and are expecting to put a boarding crew on it within the hour."

"Well, in a way I'm glad," Hammond replied. "Maybe now I will have some help making out all the reports that go with detaining a Japanese vessel. For a while there I had visions of doing all the work myself, and even for these two vessels it is going to be no easy task. You just can't believe the amount of forms that will have to be filled out."

As the discussion progressed, the two walked over to the chart table. Capt. Forsterer pointed out how it had been quite impossible for the other two Japanese vessels to get past the *Burton Island*. He indicated on the chart where the *Burton Island* had been south of the fleeing fishermen and had thus cut off their escape. It had really been fortunate that the icebreaker had been on its way north, and therefore in the right position to intercept.

Forsterer hadn't realized so much time had passed when Lt. jg Jones approached to inform him that the second fishing boat was to be intercepted within a couple of hours at the pace they were presently closing the gap. Equipped with that information, the captain passed the word for the second boarding party to be alerted and for the gunners and the signalmen to be on the ready.

The captain smiled inwardly to think that the whole thing was coming off with no more hitches than there had been up to this point. Well, he thought, the next couple of hours will tell what kind of an overall operation this was going to be. With that thought in mind he dismissed Hammond saying, "I suppose you will want to get ready for the boarding, won't you?"

"There she is over there," Jones said as he pointed to the fishing boat gradually becoming more visible dead ahead, as had been indicated both on the radar and by one of the lookouts.

"Swing her over a little so we will have them on our port side," Capt. Forsterer said to the helmsman as they proceeded closer. "I don't want the surfboat to go any farther than it has to."

"They appear to be dead in the water, sir," Lt. Jones said, but the captain was already walking out onto the port wing to oversee the launching of the second boarding party. Looking down, he could see that everything was going as smoothly as it had with the first party. The fishing boat some 500 yards off was rising and falling on the waves, with very little if any activity aboard that he could see.

He wondered if anyone on the fishing boat could read the messages the signalmen above him were blinking out. As he listened to the clicking of the signal lamp he watched through his glasses. For a brief moment he thought he could see activity on the bridge of the vessel, but from that distance he couldn't be sure of what, if anything, it meant.

"Give Lt. Stracener a call and tell him to stand by where he is," the captain said, really not to anyone in particular. Then he added, "No point in them continuing this way."

Lt. Jones tried several times to reach the *Maru No. 8* on the walkie-talkie but without success. He turned to the captain who was now deep in thought. "I can't seem to get an answer from them. I believe we have moved out of the walkie-talkie range."

In the captain's mind there wasn't much chance that there would be resistance with this boarding, because, he reasoned, it would have happened with the first boat if it were going to happen. He really didn't know whether he would enjoy firing a shot across their bow or not. He knew down deep that he damned well would do it to show them that he meant business, but it would be better if they just gave up peacefully. He really didn't want any of his men hurt, and certainly if there were resistance there was a chance someone would get hurt.

It's much better this way, he told himself as he watched the boarding party clamber onto the deck and disappear into different portions of the ship where their assignments took them.

"Everything is secure over there," Lt. Jones called to him.

"Let me have that," Capt. Forsterer said, meaning the walkie-talkie, as he approached Jones back in the pilothouse.

"Ensign Conway, I want you guys to do the best you can to get them to open up as to where their nets are," the captain stated as he depressed the button on the piece. "I don't know what you will have to tell them to get the information out of them, but give it a good try. Now, as soon as we get started you fall in behind us. We know that that vessel will go about ten knots so we'll hold our speed down so you can keep up." With that he handed the instrument back to Lt. Jones, saying, "Don't forget to tell Lt. Stracener the same thing about the nets again, when he gets into earshot."

Jones nodded that he understood, then focused his attention on the fishing boat as the captain was doing.

"I'm going down to the radio room to see what is happening with the *Burton Island*. As soon as the boat is back and loaded, get us underway," Capt. Forsterer said, "holler if you need me for anything."

Jones watched as the captain disappeared down the ladder to the deck below, wondering why he didn't take this opportunity to get himself something to eat. While the captain might not have realized it, Jones knew that it had been early morning since the commanding officer had had anything to eat. The subject had been mentioned several times, and he had sent for a sandwich at one time. But even after it had been delivered, it had gone untouched. It still sat on the chart table where it had been originally placed. The coffee that had accompanied it had long since been drunk, but the sandwich remained.

Lt. Jones was still looking at the sandwich out of the corner of his eye, wondering what he should do about it, if anything, when the captain returned to the bridge.

"Well, things are going nicely with the *Burton Island*, so we have done about all the damage we can. We're to escort these two back to the nets. The *Citrus* is steaming out of Kodiak and will be waiting for us at the net area. One of the C-130's dropped a radio marker down near one to help them locate the area." Lt. Jones was looking at the captain's face while he listened, trying to get some idea as to whether the captain considered it good or bad news. Failing in this, he just toyed with a button on the front of his shirt and awaited the captain's move.

"Have you been able to raise the *Maru No. 8?*" inquired the captain.

"I was about to try them now, sir," Jones replied.

"Let me see if I can," he said, taking the walkie-talkie from Jones and backing over to the starboard wing, hoping that might give him more range on the equipment.

"I've reached them, and I told them to reverse course. They can only go about eight knots so it'll be a while before we catch up with them. They'll be heading back toward the net area. Have radar keep you posted and give them a wide berth when you go around them. We don't need another close call like the first one. Ensign Conway will be behind you, so keep him posted too when you start getting close to them." The captain seemed a little pleased with himself and the way things were progressing. After all, it had been good news to hear that the *Burton Island* was placing a prize crew on the other two boats and would soon be heading for the net area. Now all they had to do was convince those Japanese that the jig was up and they might as well pick up their nets. He had to admit to himself that for a time he would have liked to have captured all four of the fishing vessels, but now that he had two under his wing he believed that was quite enough.

When he glanced down and saw the untouched sandwich, he began to realize just how hungry he was. "I think I'll head down for a bit to eat, and I'll be in my cabin if anything develops that I should know."

As he passed other crew members in the passageway, he tried to think back to how long it had been since he had eaten, and the more he thought about the length of time it had been, the hungrier he became. As he passed the radio room the amount of activity caused his curiosity to overcome his hunger pangs, and he went in.

"Sounds like more orders," he said as he moved up behind "Sparks" and looked down to the message he was writing.

The radio operator finished the message before he turned to Capt. Forsterer saying, "Juneau headquarters is trying to reach a Japanese enforcement vessel to come to Kodiak and take charge of their wayward ones. The *Clover* has been instructed to relieve the *Burton Island's* boarding crews and escort the two. The *Burton Island* will continue on her original patrol."

"Send the message on up to Lt. Jones," the captain said, "I just have to get myself something to eat." With that he turned and left the room.

The first thing he said when he encountered his steward was, "You better put me on a good steak and a couple of eggs, I'm hungry as hell."

The captain started to lie down on the bunk but thought better of it. Boy, he told himself, as tired as I am if I lie down I'll be sound asleep when he brings my vittles.

The steward hadn't questioned the meal order. While he had no way of knowing the captain hadn't eaten the sandwich that had been sent up, he knew it had been an awfully long time since he had eaten anything substantial.

14. NO HELP

By now the cutter had completely moved out of their view and was apparently up to full speed as they moved through the fog. Lt. Stracener walked over to where the ship's log was lying. He opened the book trying to determine the correct date, then following the last entry he wrote: "13 July 1972 this vessel has been taken into custody by the U.S.C.G. Cutter *Wachusett* for violation of the I.N.P.F.C. Agreement. Vessel taken into custody 138-828Y (49) at position 53 degrees 11 minutes north and 153.00 west, position determined by U.S.C.G. Cutter *Wachusett.*" He signed the notation Lt. Robert Stracener.

While he was sure none of the three Japanese knew what he had entered into the log, it was apparent they did not approve of any notations because all three glared at him when he turned. He walked over to what he was sure was their Long Range Radio Aid to Navigation, which appeared to be an interpretation of an American LORAN, type A. He looked the instrument over for a means of turning it on, but was interrupted by the radio operator who was just shaking his head in a negative manner. Then to make his point he broke a pencil, hoping the Coast Guard officer would get the message that the instrument was broken.

Rather than take the Japanese's word for it, the lieutenant started checking the wiring. It took very little effort to discover the aid was not plugged into a power source, therefore had no chance of operating. It proved to be a simple matter to determine what the ship's position was after turning the equipment on and sending out the electronic impulses. These figures he also entered in the logbook, under obvious protest from the Japanese officers.

It was about that time the walkie-talkie came alive again. Lt. Stracener picked the instrument up and placed it to his ear. Even as he was listening he remarked how faint the message was becoming.

"Apparently they are moving out of walkie-talkie range," he commented, then added, "they want us to make a stab at talking these people into getting the other fishing boats to stop. Maybe we can convince them they don't have a chance to get away."

Stracener leaned back against the rear bulkhead after laying the walkie-talkie down. He was not at all troubled by the fact that they were no longer in walkie-talkie range. He had expected to hear some harsh words from the cutter's commanding officer after the close call they had, and possibly with things happening as fast as they must be aboard the cutter, the whole incident might be forgotten by the next time they were in range. He knew that he would never bring the matter up himself, and he just hoped that no one else would either.

"That's one hell of a powerful radar outfit," Glass said to the lieutenant as he nodded toward the gear. "It's far more sophisticated than that aboard the *Wachusett.*" Glass was commenting on the gear more to draw him out than anything else.

"Yes, it does appear to be more up to date than anything we have on the cutter," Lt. Stracener answered. "But what concerns me more right now is the fact that both Dempsey and Franklin seem to be deathly sick. I have never known them to be seasick before. Have you?"

As Glass moved over to where the lieutenant was looking out the window at the two on deck, he said, "No, I can't say as I have, but the roll of this thing is far different than anything that I have ever experienced before."

"You know, I hadn't noticed it till now, maybe because of the other excitement. I'll have to agree with you though about this thing. There just doesn't seem to be any rhyme or reason to the pitching and rolling this vessel goes through. She acts just like she was a cork—first we go one way and then the other, with no way of predicting which will be next. Rather weird, I'd say."

"Well, from the look of things those two aren't going to be of any value to us in their present condition," Glass said as he nodded in their direction. The other two members of the boarding party were leaning over the rail emptying their stomachs into the sea. Even from that distance it was obvious that neither was in the least bit concerned at the moment as to whether he lived or died.

"What do you suppose those Japs are up to?" Lt. Stracener queried as he took another look down and saw several of the crew members walking by the two, watching their capers.

"What the hell are they doing?" Glass asked as he tried to see what was going on.

"Well, they just seem to be parading by like they had never seen anyone seasick before. Just doesn't make sense," the lieutenant said.

Glass elbowed the captain out of the way so he could get a good look. After watching a few minutes, he said, "You know they aren't paying any attention to Franklin, they're only interested in Dempsey. I'll just bet it's that brush heap of his that interests them."

"I'll bet you're right," Lt. Stracener answered. "They just haven't seen a beard like that one of his before."

"Yep, they think he is a real weirdo," Glass laughed.

Lt. Stracener had never thought too much about beards one way or the other; he just knew that he had never been interested in growing one. First of all, he never thought of them as becoming for officers, and it just seemed that his face felt cleaner after a good shave. But these Japanese that he had seen trying to grow a beard had usually wound up with some heavy fuzz.

Bringing himself back to things at hand, the lieutenant said, "I suppose they will have to be put back aboard the cutter as soon as we can contact them again. Doesn't make much sense to have them suffering here, if they aren't going to be able to stand any watches with us." Then after a couple of minutes he added, "However, right now we are out of walkie-talkie range, so it will just have to wait."

"Well as long as this tub keeps pitching when it should roll, and rolling when it should list, I don't suppose those guys will ever be anything but sick," Glass said, beginning to feel sorry for the two.

"There is always hope that they will become accustomed to the motion of the ship. I sure hope so, because we could sure use their help to stand watches," the lieutenant explained.

"I rather doubt that either of them will be able to stand any watches tonight, by the look of things," Glass commented.

"No, I suppose not. I imagine that we will have to take turns tonight," Stracener replied. "Maybe they will feel better in the morning."

"I wouldn't make any bets on their condition being any better in the morning," Glass said.

"I have a feeling that we could be on this boat for some time. After all, it isn't very fast, even though it does have a fast getaway," the lieutenant said, adding, "it could be tough going if we have to stand all the watches between the two of us, and don't get any help." Then as he adjusted his gunbelt for the hundredth time, he looked around at the three Japanese who were still in the pilothouse. The darned gun felt awfully uncomfortable but he didn't believe that he was ready to give up the security it offered. By the look of the captain and the radioman there might be no need for the gun anymore, but there was just nowhere that he felt he wanted to put it, at least not at the present time. The fish manager certainly did not appear to be one to be trusted.

"Now that things have quieted down a little, why don't you try another shot with those 'Tri-Language' cards?" Glass asked. "Maybe they have learned to read since we tried before." As he said it he removed the deck of cards from his pocket and nodded to the radioman and the captain to look them over. He didn't try to include the fish manager because he didn't feel that they would receive any cooperation from him. He couldn't really put his finger on why he felt that way, but there was that feeling.

Both Japanese seemed to be eyeing the .45 automatics Glass and Lt. Stracener were carrying on their hips more than they were the cards. It was evident that both were very ill at ease and handled the cards very gingerly.

After a few tries it was clear to Glass that he wasn't getting anyplace with them; they wouldn't admit that they knew even one of the words depicted on the cards. He finally just threw up his hands and said, "Well, do you want to give it a try?"

"I don't think that I will be able to do any better, but I did see a blackboard down below a while ago. I don't remember exactly where, but maybe Franklin does; he was with me. Why don't you get that and maybe we can get through to them with that and a few pictures," the lieutenant said.

Glass made no reply but merely turned and headed for the door of the pilothouse. Even as he started down the steps to the deck he realized that it was important that the lieutenant stay on the bridge to make sure that the fishing boat continued on the course that had been set. While he doubted in his own mind that the Japanese would try to change course there was no point in their encouraging the move.

He flipped the collar of his jacket up as he cleared the shelter of the cabin, receiving the full blast of the wind and rain. He looked up hoping to see a break in the clouds, but none was visible, and thus the chance of clearing weather was not very likely.

"Say, did either of you fellows see a blackboard down here any place?" Glass asked as he passed where Franklin was now lying on the deck. The wind and rain seemed to be completely ignored by the sick man.

"I think we saw it in the aft cabin when we were making our inspection tour," the sick Coastie said with pain visible in his face.

"Why don't you get inside out of the weather?" Glass asked, as he was forced to grab onto a railing to keep his balance. The vessel had just made another of its unpredictable rolls. "After all, there isn't any point in getting wet," he continued as he attempted to figure how wet the two must be already from their exposure.

"Good garsh," Frankling replied, "if I could find a spot on this tub that didn't smell to high heaven with fish, just maybe I could keep my stomach in place."

Now that he thought of it, Glass realized that the whole ship did smell pretty strong of dead fish. He really hadn't paid much attention to it before but he could rationalize that anyone with the least bit of a weak stomach would have problems with that smell. Now he wondered why it hadn't been noticeable to him before. It was just a good thing he didn't have a weak gut he thought. With that he headed for the aft cabin in search of the blackboard. It didn't take a great deal of rummaging to find the board, which was leaning against the bulkhead just inside the door.

On his way back with the board under one arm he addressed the two again, "Say, does either one of you fellows do any drawing?" Then before either of them could answer, he added, "we may be able to use you fellows. We're trying to get through to those damned Japanese and we haven't found a way yet. Just maybe if you get out of this rain and get your mind off your troubles you will feel better."

It was apparent that neither agreed with his idea but both were willing to give it a try. On the way back to the bridge, Dempsey admitted that he had studied mechanical drawing while in high school and would do his best to come up with some type of drawings, if it would help.

Glass wanted badly to say something about Dempsey and his beard, and how it was such an attraction for the Japanese crew members, but after seeing how sick he appeared to be, abandoned the idea. The three paraded up the steps to the pilothouse without a word being spoken.

15. NEW QUARTERS

"Geez, you'll have them believing that the entire Coast Guard
fleet is in on this caper," Glass said as he surveyed the drawings
of ships and planes that Dempsey had drawn on the blackboard.
None of the prize crew realized at that time that there were two
additional Coast Guard vessels ready to take part. As far as they
knew, the *Citrus* and themselves were the extent of the operation. The *Burton Island* and the *Clover* had not been mentioned
when they left the *Wachusett*.

"Well, if we can get them to believe that the balance of their
fleet doesn't have a ghost of a chance of getting away, just maybe we can get them to radio them to give up," Lt. Stracener said
as he motioned for the Japanese who were now in the cabin to
take a good look at the drawing.

The Japanese trio began chattering away with periodic pointing at the drawing, and shaking of their heads. This went on for
some time and the Guardsmen began to wonder if they had got
through to them or not. After what seemed like hours the radioman indicated that he would like to try sending a message.

The lieutenant was more than willing to let him use the gear,
and after he made it known, a few buttons were flipped and the
operator picked up the mike. After he had picked it up as
though he were going to talk into it, he again turned to the
other two for a few more words of instruction. When he considered himself ready, he spoke into the mike, and his comments

were rather brief to start. But after a long flood of Japanese pouring from the receiver, he went back at it. There was no way for the Coasties to tell what the message was that he had transmitted, nor what the replies were from the other end. After several minutes of listening, the operator flipped the buttons again and both the receiver and transmitter went dead.

"I don't think we made the grade," Lt. Stracener said as he eyed the operator and then the others after the call.

"I'm inclined to agree with you," Glass replied. "Maybe if we can find a way to convey to them it will cost them more money in fines if they continue to make a run for it, we may get some results."

The drawings on the board took on a different tack, as Dempsey tried to pass the new message on. He had been at it for some time before the Japanese seemed to grasp the meaning all at the same time.

Again the radio operator warmed up his equipment, and the conversation in Japanese was hot and heavy. There was little question as to what was being said this time because the operator would continually point out something on the blackboard just as though the person he was communicating with was able to see it. It didn't seem to make much difference on the other end for several minutes, then a smile crossed the operator's face. With a broad smile he bowed to the four Guardsmen and then went back to transmitting for a spell. He didn't even bother to look at his captain or the fish company manager, as he silenced the radio and stepped back against the rear bulkhead.

"Say, I do believe we hit pay dirt," Lt. Stracener remarked, turning to their artist and thanking him for his efforts.

"As long as we have them going, why don't we try to find out why they didn't do as the patrol planes asked—like proceeding to Kodiak after all the planes said they saw them pick up the messages?" Glass chimed in.

Back to the drawing board went Dempsey and a new set of pictures developed with planes swooping down on fishing boats and pictures of fishermen picking messages out of the sea. It just didn't matter what the pictures depicted, none of the Japanese would give any indication that they had seen or heard an airplane of any kind. Regardless of how many drawings, or what type of plane they were, patrol or helicopter, the Japanese were not admitting they knew anything about the matter. They certainly gave the impression they were not going to admit they picked up any messages if they would not even admit they had seen any airplanes.

After close to an hour of drawings and re-drawings, the four were forced to admit defeat, and the effort was abandoned.

"Say," Lt. Stracener said at length, after looking intently at the radar screen for a time, "we have two ships on the screen now, and it appears that we are gaining on them, and the only way we could gain on anyone at this speed is that they are standing still, or barely moving."

"I sure as hell hope we are catching up," Glass said in reply. "I would hate to think that we were going to be chasing them all the way to Japan."

"I believe our little chalk-talk session brought us some results," the lieutenant broke in. "Now if we can just get close enough so this walkie-talkie can reach them, we can find out what the whole story is."

As Lt. Stracener kept his eyes glued to the radar screen and the dots became larger and larger, he continued to try to reach the bridge of the *Wachusett*, but more than an hour passed before he could even get some crackling noises from it.

It was during the wait that the Japanese took their turn on the drawing board. Hand signals and drawings continued without the invaders paying a great deal of attention. Only after the Japanese became insistent did the four start observing what they were doing! After about a half hour of playing charades with them, the message came through loud and clear.

"I do believe they are trying to tell us that they are short on drinking water," Lt. Stracener said, "and it looks like they are afraid that if we drink or expect to wash, they are not going to have enough for themselves."

"Shee-it! They don't have to worry about me drinking any of their water if they have beer aboard," Glass said as he took over the drawing board and tried to convey the message that he was interested in a bottle of beer.

He didn't have to work too long before the radio operator disappeared for a short time. When he returned he was carrying a can of beer, and this he turned over to Glass with bow.

Glass returned the bow, and with a big, cheery smile on his face he downed the beer in nothing flat. Handing back the empty can he bowed some more, hoping it would indicate that if there were more he wouldn't be so impolite as to refuse it.

It worked. The Japanese returned with two more cans. Glass offered one of the cans to his fellow crew members and Lt. Stracener, but wasn't the least displeased when they refused. In no time at all the cans were empty, but additional bowing failed to have the desired effect. The Japanese just ignored him.

"You sure that isn't going to make you drunk?" Lt. Stacener asked, showing a great deal of concern as to whether he would be able to depend on him until the effects might wear off. Right at that point he still felt that he desperately needed at least one hand to help with the chores. He knew he would be unable to depend a great deal on the other two in their sickly condition.

"Hell, three cans of beer aren't going to even wet my whistle. And, from the signs this Jap is giving me, that's all the beer they have on this tub," Glass said, adding, "Maybe I had better go down and check those ALPAT boxes that the fisheries people put up for occasions such as this. There must be some water packed. Surely they wouldn't expect us to drink whatever we were to find here."

"Good idea," the lieutenant said, as he turned back to check the blips on the radar screen, trying to determine whether it was worth the effort to try the walkie-talkie again just then.

"I'll help Glass with the box," Franklin said as he went out the door behind Glass. He wasn't really interested in helping, but he was eager to get out into the fresh air with hopes it would clear his head a bit, even if it didn't soothe his stomach. The closeness of the cabin had made him near to the point of emptying his stomach more than once during those chalk-talks. He had gritted his teeth and would have left much sooner if he could have come up with any kind of excuse.

He envied Glass as he watched him cross the deck as though the rolling ship meant nothing at all. It took every bit of strength he could muster just to keep standing, let alone pacing around as Glass was.

There wasn't any trouble finding the ALPAT box. It was still sitting on the deck exactly where it had been thrown when the boarding crew had landed, some three to four hours before.

Glass grabbed the box, flipped off the catch, and jerked the top open on the three-by-four-foot blue wooden box. Franklin didn't show much enthusiasm; he just stood back and watched as the contents were scattered out on deck. In addition to the box, there were four sleeping bags that had also been thrown aboard, but neither of the men figured anything would have been packed in them so they were left intact. In the box there were three cartons of "C" rations, which would actually be enough to last one person about 24 hours, but certainly not enough for the four of them.

"Geez," Glass said, "they don't figure we are going to be very hungry, do they?" He displayed the three small cartons for Franklin to see.

"Look, you can sure as hell have my share. I couldn't hold that crap down if I felt good, let alone the way I feel now," was the reply.

"These packages are supposed to be arranged by experts," Glass continued, more or less ignoring Franklin's reply. "All I can say is that they must have taken the toilet accommodations into considertion; then, using Einstein's theory of $E = MC^2$, concluded that if you don't eat you don't need a toilet."

"Ah, cut the jokes," Franklin said. "Is there any water?"

"Relax, I'm sure there will be a package here marked 'Instant Water.' Just add water and stir," Glass replied, still rummaging around in the box. "Ah, here we are. Some 16-ounce cans that have been taken from a Coast Guard life raft. Maybe a good thing they didn't leave that part to those Fisheries creeps."

"Well, as long as we have some water those Japs won't be so worried," Franklin said. "I'll go up and tell the lieutenant and he can pass the word to the Japs." With that he started back toward the pilothouse.

Glass called to him, "Take a couple of these sleeping bags with you; there isn't much point in letting them get all wet out here."

After having thought of the toilet facilities that might be available, Glass decided that this would be a good time to check the matter out. He went through the motions of squatting to the first Japanese fisherman he saw, also displaying a roll of toilet paper. The Japanese looked at the roll as though it was something completely foreign to him. Then, after opening it and getting a better look, he decided he knew what it was. The message Glass had been trying to convey was interpreted. The fisherman pointed out a small cubby-hole type closet that apparently served as the head for the entire crew.

Glass swung the door open, expecting to see something at least as large as a telephone booth, but it wasn't that large. Inside, there was a trough you were expected to back up to. The motion of the rolling ship served as the means of flushing. The thing would still have been all right it if had been constructed for even a fair-sized man, but it wasn't. Even by pulling his pants down in advance there was just no way that he could squeeze himself in. After a few tries he gave it up as a bad job.

What the hell do I do now, Glass thought as he backed up and surveyed the situation again. There just wasn't any question in his mind but that he was going to have to do something about it, and soon.

By now there were a couple of fishermen standing around wondering just what the American would do next. Even though it wasn't all that obvious, Glass just knew they wanted to have a good laugh at his expense, but he wasn't going to let that happen. So, to keep them from thinking he wasn't capable of handling the situation, he headed back toward the fantail of the ship with the paper in his hand. He had barely got started with his chore when Lt. Stracener rounded the corner of the aft cabin. "What in heaven's name are you trying to do, fall overboard?" the lieutenant asked, not noticing anything except the fact that Glass was leaning far overboard.

"I'd say it should be pretty obvious what I'm doing," Glass shot back, adding, "have you seen the size of the head?" and concluding with, "they must recruit nothing but midgets for crew members. There just doesn't seem to be anything big enough here for a full-sized man."

Realizing that Glass might like some privacy, Lt. Stacener headed back around the cabin but drew up short after rounding the corner with the thought that he had better stick around a bit and make sure that Glass didn't fall overboard. With that he slipped back where he could keep an eye on him.

He was as glad as Glass when the task was completed, each of course for different reasons. Stracener just didn't know what he was going to do when his time came; he didn't know if he would be able to go through the antics that Glass did. He decided that he would just have to work something out when the time came. Heading back for the pilothouse, he hoped that he could get through on the walkie-talkie now; they must be getting close enough.

Glass was in no hurry to return to the pilothouse. After all, they had got the Japanese to communicate with the other ships, and as far as they knew everything was as close to O.K. as they were going to get.

As he wandered around, he began to feel the effects of the tension that he had gone through before and during the boarding. Now that he thought about it a little more, he knew that he had been scared at the time, but it had been one of those things that you do whether you want to or not. Now that it was over he felt nervous, not so much with what he thought might take place now but with what could well have happened before. Oh, well, he figured, the feeling is bound to wear off in a little while and he would just have to ignore it. With that he continued a preliminary inspection of the ship.

16. AN ESCAPE?

Fish Manager Hio Yokoma wandered around the deck of the fishing boat in an attempt to keep on eye on the lanky young Coastie. At one point it appeared there would be one less intruder because it looked as though the Coastie would fall overboard. No one could lean that far forward over the fantail without eventually losing his grip, but that Coastie seemed to prove that it was possible. Now the guy was wandering around the vessel again and that was a real concern.

He had managed to keep their engineer in hiding so far but he didn't know how much longer the fellow could stay out of sight. He was sure in his own mind that if their engineer was to come into contact with one of the Coastie, it wouldn't take them long to learn that he could speak English. The young fellow was just working this fishing boat between terms at the University of Tokyo and was said to be pretty good with his English. So far they had convinced the Coast Guardsmen no one aboard could speak or understand their language, and he would like to keep it that way as long as possible. He was sure he could continue to work on an escape plan, as long as there was no real communication between the intruders and the fishermen.

That damned, lanky straight-eye had been actually making friends with the radio man, Charlie, and had made friendly overtures to other fishermen. Even the captain didn't seem man enough to know that the Coast Guardsmen were only pretending friendship in order to use them. Couldn't they realize it was the same thing with the occupation forces stationed in Japan, who had fooled a great many of his countrymen with so-called friendship? While they had fooled a lot of women and some of the younger men, they had never fooled him with that line. They had even brought over their engineers and other craftsmen, supposedly to build up Japan's economy, teaching Japanese to build cars and so on. How in the world did they think Japan ever made it into a position of one of the world's industrial powers before the war if they didn't have their own know-how?

He breathed a sigh of relief as he watched the officer head back for the pilothouse. Now if he could just get the lanky one to quit nosing around he would feel better.

He was sorry that he had conceded and gone along with the idea of radioing one of the other fishing vessels to stop for the Coast Guard. At the time, it appeared there was no chance of their escaping, and he was sure in his own mind that it would be easier for two vessels to stage an escape than it would be for just one. The odds seemed to favor one of them making it because the cutter just couldn't chase both of them at the same time, and aircraft would be of little use during the dark hours of the night. He had thought it would be closer to nightfall when the three vessels made a group, but now it appeared they would be on their way toward Kodiak a couple hours before dark, and that would mean additional running before they reached the abstention line.

Naturally it was his hope it would be the boat he was on that would make good in the escape because he was the head man of the fishing expedition; the others should be willing to make some sacrifice to allow him to go free.

He surely wished that he knew exactly how fast that cutter could go. If, a few hours ago, they had been in a position to intercept, that would have been altogether different from being capable of catching them. After all, he reflected, we had been zigzagging into as many fog banks as possible when they were running and that fact no doubt contributed to our capture. This time they would take a straight course, thus saving a great many miles. All the information he had picked up regarding the Coast Guard patrol vessels indicated that the buoy tenders and icebreakers were only capable of about eight knots, and the Japanese could go that fast. This cutter that had caught them was something he knew nothing about.

He wasn't sure exactly what they would do with the Guardsmen once they made good their escape. Of course, they could say the Coast Guard had been wrong about where the boarding had taken place. There were lots of things they could say, but that problem could be taken care of later; he was sure of that.

They were still proceeding away from Kodiak and would continue to until they contacted the second fishing boat. The longer that took the better off he felt they were, because they would be that much closer to that abstention line, and then a break for it wouldn't take as much running. He was sure in his own mind that if they were able to once get across that line the Coast Guard would give up the chase. Oh, sure, they might file a protest with the Japanese Government, but he had heard of such protests before. Just reply that the Coast Guardsmen must have made another of their mistakes because he wouldn't direct vessels under his supervision to violate the law. He would merely remind the Japanese authorities that it was another attempt by the Coast Guard to create problems for the Japanese fishermen. It had worked for him before so why wouldn't it work again?

He continued to rationalize to himself that with sundown things would be different. Two of the Coast Guardsmen they had aboard would certainly offer little trouble; they were too busy with their seasickness. The officer and the lanky one were not both going to be able to stay awake all night, so there would really be only one to contend with when the time was ripe.

He was sure he could put enough pressure on the captain to get his cooperation in the attempt. Charlie had just better change his ideas about working with the Coast Guard and quit his silly argument about things would go easier on them if they didn't resist. He was going to keep in mind how easily that radio operator had been sold a bill of goods by those Guardsmen, and he just might make it difficult for the guy to get another job in the future. What right had he to argue in favor of cooperation with them anyway?

He was not going to allow the Yokoma name to be tarnished by his being hauled into Kodiak for illegal fishing. What would his family have to say about something as disgraceful as that? They wouldn't think anything of the fact that he was fishing illegally in U.S. waters, but the thought that he had allowed himself to be caught was disgraceful and really would be inexcusable in their eyes. No, he was just going to have to make good his escape.

He knew his mother would be shamed if he were to return to Japan under arrest. She was still too proud of the fact that his father had preferred death to surrendering the aircraft carrier he had commanded all through World War II. It had been the fact that his family name was Yokoma that had permitted him to attend the Japan Naval College toward the end of the war. He had been real young when he entered, but it had been what he had dreamed of doing from the time he could remember anything. The class he was in had graduated early because of the great need for naval officers. While he wasn't given command of the destroyer he first went aboard, he knew that if the war continued he would have his own ship soon. The men under him had complained to others that he was too strict, but they never dared question one of his orders to his face. There were times when he really wished that one would. If it had happened, he was certain that he would have made an example for the others never to question another order of his.

He had never admitted that the United States had defeated his country, and even now he blamed them for having cut short his naval career. Following the war, the Japanese Navy had been reduced to just a token force, thus making him seek another means of support. This had happened even though the Yokoma name had been synonymous with Japanese naval activity almost since the original ships flew the flag with the "Rising Sun" on it.

He could well recall those unfortunate days. He had thought seriously about moving to the Philippines at the time. He had heard there were still Japanese fighting there—men who refused to believe Japan had been defeated—and he would have liked to join them. He would have if the Americans hadn't put a stop to all overseas travel by Japanese at the time. It was then that he realized that if he were to continue his life connected with activities relative to the sea it would have to be aboard a fishing boat. Sure, some of the other officers had bowed and scraped for the Americans and had been allowed to continue on as tugboat personnel or the like, but he could never see himself bowing for them regardless of the rewards or penalties.

Damn that Coast Guardsman, Yokoma said to himself as he watched Glass head into the after cabin door. How in the devil would he keep him from seeing the engineer?

Yokoma slipped into the cabin behind Glass as inconspicuously as he could. The first person he encountered he grabbed by the shoulder saying, "Get that engineer out of sight. I don't want this Coast Guardsman seeing him." Yokoma was not the least bit concerned whether Glass heard him giving the order or not; he was that sure the Coastie could not understand Japanese. The fisherman he issued the order to lost no time in its execution because he could see the determination on Yokoma's face.

The fish manager watched as Glass looked through cabinets and closets. What he was searching for he couldn't figure out. The Coastie had looked over their rifles used for killing sharks and had ignored them as well as the ammunition that was stored with them. Without being interested in guns or ammo, what was there left to seek out?

As he continued to keep his eye on Glass, he recalled the fishing boats he had been compelled to search while serving on the destroyer in Philippine waters. The senior officers had been concerned because occasionally a disguised fishing boat would be carrying radio equipment and passing on ship movements to the American Navy. If his destroyer captain felt they had time for a search, Yokoma was likely as not in charge of the boarding party. They never conducted a search in the manner this Coastie was doing. Yokoma had taught his men to be generous in the use of their gun butts, as well as the barrel. A few broken ribs or jaws among the fishermen being searched usually speeded things along, and it certainly did bring them to attention much faster.

On occasions when it wasn't feasible timewise for a search, they would merely give their gunnery crew some target practice, or the destroyer would run the fishing boats down. They never bothered with survivors; it was a waste of time and necessitated feeding them until they could reach port again. The thought of one of his men wandering around a fishing boat all by himself, such as this Coast Guardsman was doing, would have been certain grounds for disciplinary action, if the fellow hadn't got himself killed in the meantime. The more he thought about it the more he approved of this fellow's action. The Coastie had some time ago put his .45 automatic back into its holster and fastened the clasp. If he were to run into trouble, it would be all over for him before he could get the gun out, and that was certainly in Yokoma's favor.

The more Yokoma thought about the unmilitary like manners of the Coast Guard boarding crew, the more he wondered if he shouldn't bring his engineer forward. He could have the young fellow find out what the speed of the cutter was; thus he would have a better knowledge of what their chances of escape were. He didn't dwell on the idea long though, telling himself that he had already made up his mind that there was going to be an escape attempt regardless of the speed of the cutter. Why bother finding out what the speed was? He was already relieved to see how haphazardly they were keeping affairs on the *Maru No. 8* under control. It certainly wouldn't be this way if he was the officer in charge of the crew, and they could be sure of that.

He still boiled a little as he thought of the captain bowing and bowing to the members of the boarding crew when they had first come aboard. It really sickened him to think that the captain would lower himself to that regardless of what they had done. What had it gained him?

He admitted to himself that the younger generation of Japanese were far too willing to accept Western influence in the homeland, and some Japanese companies were even investing money in the United States. A good example, he thought, was the lack of resistance when the Coast Guard had come aboard a few hours earlier. None of the younger fishermen had offered any real resistance. Surely they could have bumped at least one overboard and that would have kept the rest busy trying to fish him out of the water. This in turn could have allowed the second fishing boat additional time to make good their run for cover. These younger guys seemed far too easy to appease. This could never have happened a few years ago. Regardless of the size of the cannon on the cutter, the older Japanese would have resisted any type of boarding. As he thought about that cannon on the forward deck of the cutter, he had to admit it appeared impressive enough pointed in their direction. However, he doubted very much that the skipper of the cutter would have used it. It would have caused one hell of an international incident, and these Americans were a prissy lot when someone called their bluff, and he was sure it was a bluff.

Good, Yokoma said to himself, as he saw Glass heading back to the pilothouse. Now he could get to work setting up some type of escape plan. He knew if anything was to be done about escaping it was up to him. He could make excuses for the captain, because the man had never been anything more than a fisherman, even in the war years. He had more or less inherited the occupation from his father, and probably his father's father had been the same. You really couldn't expect a fisherman to think like a military man, and it would take the brains of a military mind to get them out of this mess.

Charlie was of the younger generation, the ones who were willing to allow the Americans to think they were an equal race. The radio operator was fairly smart, he thought, but he certainly didn't seem to be anyone he could depend on to help map out some escape strategy. Of course, the other crew members would be forced to do what they were told or it would be the last time they shipped aboard any fishing boat out of Kushiro harbor.

The way he read the signs it was going to have to be his baby —the planning all his, and the execution spearheaded by him if the project was going to get off the ground at all. The one thing he was sure of was the fact that something had to be done, and it would have to be done shortly after dark.

17. CAMPING OUT

"I've made a complete check of this tub, Lieutenant, and I can't find any place that I would care to sleep," Glass said as he returned to the bridge after a complete check below decks. Before the officer could answer him he added, "You know the only place that I found that was even half-way clean was their engineroom, and you can bet money whoever their engineer is he loves his work, because the engine is really polished up."

"Why don't we take over those three bunks in this place?" Lt. Stracener answered, indicating the three bunks in the aft portion of the pilothouse. "I have already suggested to the captain that we would be wanting them," he said. At the time he had passed the message on he had been thinking of the night watches. He knew at the time he did not want to be standing watch with one of the Japanese on the bridge, knowing that there would be two other Japanese either asleep in the room or getting prepared to jump him when his back was turned.

Before he had finished the statement, Glass was opening the door to the back room. Stracener didn't make any move to stop him; he was sure that Glass was merely going in to pick out a bunk for himself, and that was all right with him. By all indications it would be just the two of them who would be standing the watches, at least for tonight.

Lt. Stracener was momentarily startled when he realized Glass was standing right beside him when he said, "Hell, have you tried laying down in one of those bunks? They are just too damned short for me. I wouldn't be able to get five minutes' rest all cramped up like that." Seeing the bewildered look on the lieutenant's face, he added, "I think that I would prefer to take my sleeping bag out on the deck. I can't sleep in there and I can't stand that stink below decks."

"Suit yourself," Stracener replied, "but I think I'll still keep the room empty for the time being." He said it as though he thought Glass was going to suggest that they give the accommodations back to the captain and the companyman, Yokoma. He was almost surprised when Glass made no indication that he had been thinking of passing the room back to the Japanese.

At that point the radio operator very timidly tapped Lt. Stracener on the shoulder and beckoned toward the radio equipment as though he wanted to use it. He picked up the microphone as though he were making a call, and then kept repeating "Mama San" as though that was whom he would like to call, but only with the lieutenant's permission.

His chin dropped down on his chest when Stracener shook his head and repeated "No" several times. There was little doubt that the operator was crushed by the denial.

"Well, here we go again," Glass said as he moved back to allow another one of the Japanese crew members to enter the small pilothouse.

"What do you mean?" Stracener asked as he looked around to see what Glass was referring to, then said, "Oh, one of them," and watched unimpressed as the crew member extended his hands as though he were wearing handcuff. His feet were also close together indicating the position of having leg irons on. He repeated a couple of times what had now become an old story, "Mama San, Papa San, Baby San." With that he bowed and turned to leave.

"Do you suppose someone down below decks is rehearsing those clowns so they can come up here and put on that act?" Glass asked as the man left.

"Sure as the world looks like it," Stracener said, adding, "What is that—about the tenth one now who has pulled that?"

"I don't know how many, but it looked like a communion line there for a while," Glass commented.

"I suppose they are looking for sympathy," Stracener said as he tried not to smile in front of the other Japanese in the room. "Why don't you check around and find a place to bed down? I think the captain and I will be taking the first watch." Stracener looked to see how Glass would receive the news that he intended to take the first watch, something that he considered his right as the senior rank in this boarding party. He was almost disappointed when Glass didn't even bother to answer but turned and left the pilothouse.

Cripe! Glass thought as he walked down the ladder to the ship's deck. If Stracener thought he was going to give him a hassle about taking the first watch, he must be crazy. He'd a hell of a lot rather have the watch when there weren't a bunch around looking over his shoulder.

As he made his way along the deck—holding tight to the railing that ran the length of the main cabin because of the unpredictable roll of the ship—he wondered what had happened to Franklin and Dempsey. He recalled now that he hadn't seen them in the last hour or so.

He didn't have long to wonder. As he stepped around the aft side of the cabin he saw that they had laid the sleeping bags behind that cabin in hope of getting out of the spray and weather to some degree. He had already thought of the spot as a likely place for his own sleeping bag but with the two of them there it didn't leave much room for anyone else. It was apparent they must have sacked out early, because they both appeared to be asleep. As he surveyed the area he was convinced that he could do better. There was still plenty of evidence of the last fish that had been caught, in the scraps lying throughout the area where their bags were down. In spite of the wind there was a strong fish odor about.

A complete tour of the main deck provided Glass with little encouragement as far as finding what he considered a decent place to put his sleeping bag. He was just about to give the whole thing up and settle for one of the short bunks, and was even headed back toward the pilothouse, when he noticed the ladder running to the top of the house. He didn't hold much hope for what he would find there, what with the spray going completely over the house on occasion, and the chance of getting out of the wind rather remote.

He walked over and leaned against the exhaust stack as he surveyed the roof of the pilothouse. As he gazed around he noticed that there was very little spray and mist hitting him here. It seemed that the exhaust shooting out the top of the stack forced the droplets to fall farther away. The stack even offered a measure of warmth. Yep, he had found the spot to put his sleeping bag down, just no doubt about it.

He realized just how tired he was as he climbed into the sleeping bag. He had already told Strcener where he was bunked down so the lieutenant would know where he could be found when he finished the first watch. Glass could recall the startled look on Stracener's face when he told him that he was going to be sleeping on the roof of the cabin. It probably sounded like he had flipped his cork, sleeping on the roof. Now that he was lying down it was really surprising how little of the moisture fell on him here.

It seemed as though he had barely snuggled into the bag when someone was shaking him awake. It was 2 a.m. and time for him to take over the watch. He could have slept a lot longer he knew, but that was life he figured, as he made his way to the pilothouse.

"Well, are you and I supposed to spend the rest of this beautiful morning together?" Glass inquired with a broad smile as he entered the pilothouse and noticed the radio operator was now on duty.

The operator answered with an even broader smile, "Hi. . . hi," just as though he had understood exactly what Glass had said. Glass looked hard at the Japanese and said, "Have you been trying to shit us that you couldn't understand English?" The operator got a hurt look on his face. He knew that he was being reprimanded from the Coastie's expression. Glass was the last person that he wanted to have sore at him. After all, this guardsman seemed to be the only one of the lot who showed any concern for the plight they were in.

Glass looked a little closer at Charlie now and realized that he had just been trying to be friendly with that "Hi. . .hi" bit, and without a doubt didn't have the least idea as to what was said when he came into the pilothouse.

"Say, Charlie, you sure there isn't any more beer on this tub?" Glass asked as he made signs that he wanted something to drink but not the water that was in the container they had received

earlier in the day from the *Wachusett*. He just hated the
thought of going through the entire watch without something to
wet his whistle. He was pretty certain now that Charlie, as he
had nicknamed the radio operator, didn't understand English
because he was having a great deal of difficulty getting his point
across.

Charlie knew shortly after Glass started doing his charade bit
what it was he wanted. The only reason he was stalling was because he would have liked to help him but he didn't have any
idea where there was anything more to drink on the boat, and
the harder he thought about it the more confusing it was to try
and come up with an answer. He certainly didn't want to
offend the guardsman but he just wasn't going to be able to help
him either.

Hell, I'm not getting anyplace with this guy, Glass told himself and started looking around. "I got it," he suddenly said
aloud, more to himself than to Charlie as he headed for the
room in back of the pilothouse. After all, he thought, if that was
the captain's quarters, there was pretty sure to be some private
stock that the skipper drank when he felt the urge.

"Just as I thought!" Glass said; again he was talking to himself, but now he couldn't see why he shouldn't say it right out
loud. If Charlie heard him he wouldn't know what it was all
about anyway. The exclamation came when he opened one of
the cupboards and found three pint-size decanter bottles. This
just had to be the captain's private stock.

It didn't take him long to uncork the first of the bottles, nor
did it take long to down the entire contents. He didn't have the
vaguest idea what the Japanese characters on the label meant,
but it certainly was one of the smoothest liquors he had ever
tasted.

He couldn't see any reason why he shouldn't drink the second
and the third bottles. After all, Charlie could handle the controls and maybe, with a little jag on, the balance of the watch
would be a bit more tolerable. He really expected that the
drinks should be starting to take effect as he closed the cupboard
and went back into the front cabin, where Charlie looked up at
him with a glance that was almost apologetic. Apparently
Charlie was sorry he didn't tell him about the captain's private
stock, Glass thought, but it didn't matter now and he slapped
Charlie on the shoulder and smiled.

"Say, Charlie, how would you like to call Mama San?" Glass
asked as he pointed to the radio equipment and motioned that it
would be all right. He had thought about doing it before, and

now that he may need the guy to take over the balance of the watch he figured it might be smart to be on the good side of him.

He had previously figured out that the radio equipment on this tub, while being quite superior, certainly didn't have the capability of reaching out as far as Japan, and for that reason he couldn't see why Lt. Stracener had denied the previous request. It sure didn't take long to get that message across to Charlie, nor it take Charlie long to warm the equipment up and start chattering into the mike. Glass had no idea what he was saying, but he was sure that Charlie was talking to members on the other fishing boats in the fleet, no doubt asking what their condition was and what they believed would be the final outcome of this mess they now found themselves in.

After nearly an hour of chattering into the mike and being answered by a great deal more chatter from the other end, Charlie shut off the equipment, turned, bowed low to the Coastie, and thanked him as best he could. Glass had an idea right then that he had made a friend. What he couldn't figure out, though, was why that liquor wasn't taking any effect at all; it just didn't make sense. Hell! he was going to have to find out what was in those bottles. It couldn't have been whiskey or he would have felt some effect by now. With that he went into the back cabin again, but this time to bring one of the decanters out with him.

He indicated to Charlie that he wanted to know what they had contained. When Charlie learned what it was Glass wanted to know, he in turn passed the word back, more by sign language than anything else, that the canisters had held cough syrup.

When the message got through, Glass just couldn't help himself and burst out laughing at his own stupidity. Then realizing that the least he could do was pass the joke on to Charlie, he did. When Charlie realized what the Coastie had done, and the fact that Glass was taking it as a joke, he too started laughing, and the more he laughed the more he felt like laughing. From that moment on there was no question but that the guardsman and the radio operator were about as good friends as were going to be made on that trip. Both Glass and Charlie knew it too, as they laughed and slapped each other on the back.

There was only one interruption during the entire watch. That was when the captain came in during the early morning hours. The two seemed to be having a tremendous argument, but because it was all taking place in Japanese, Glass didn't have the slightest idea what was taking place.

18. BOARDING PARTY SPLIT

The weather did not improve at all during the night, and dawn didn't break in that sense of the word. The fog and drizzling rain just seemed to get a little lighter as the morning wore on. None of the four Coasties realized how close they had come to finding themselves bound and possibly even gagged that morning.

Yokoma had been successful in convincing the captain that an escape attempt should be made during the night. On several occasions either the captain or Yokoma had ventured to where the Coast Guard officer was sleeping in the hope of taking his gun from him. On each occasion the officer had appeared still to be awake and the attempt to deprive him of his sidearm had to be abandoned. When the captain had made an appearance on the bridge, to convince Charlie he should take part in the caper, the captain had been turned down by the radio operator. Charlie had been quite positive in his rejection of the affair, protesting that it was foolhardy, and didn't have a possible chance of succeeding. Even if it were to succeed, Charlie argued, what chance would they have for a job on the high seas again?

The captain had been reluctant to take the news back to Yokoma, and was rather surprised to find the fury the Fish Manager was capable of displaying. He was on the verge of striking the captain for his failure to convince Charlie. In the end, he was compelled to call the thing off when he found it impossible to get close to the Coast Guard officer without the man stirring in his sleeping bag. The other two sleeping Coasties certainly didn't appear as though they would create a problem, but the officer did.

With reluctance the fish manager had agreed to put the matter off until a better opportunity presented itself.

Without knowing what happened during the night, Dempsey and Franklin were the first to arrive on the bridge, not to relieve Glass but merely to get in out of the weather. Both were soaked to the skin, and both smelled highly of fish. It was apparent the water had not only soaked through their sleeping bags, but had also soaked through their clothes to the skin, bringing the fish smell with it.

"Boy, could I ever stand a hot drink," Dempsey said, as he stood huddled in a corner of the pilothouse. "I'm soaked clean through, and I don't have any dry clothes to put on."

"As far as dry clothes are concerned, you should have brought your sea bag with you," Glass replied, "and as far as a drink goes, you find the stuff and I will be glad to share it with you. The only thing that I have found is cough syrup," and with that he broke down and told them of the cough-syrup incident.

Both Dempsey and Franklin were so miserable at the time that they failed to see much humor in it. They were far too concerned about their own plight.

When Lt. Stracener arrived on the scene, he carried the "C" rations with him, and as he tossed one package to each man he said, "Well, here is your breakfast. Eat hearty, men," in what was accepted as a mighty poor joke at the time.

Glass welcomed the bit, although he was not particularly hungry, but he did want something to take the taste of the cough syrup out of his mouth. It had been hours since he had drunk the stuff, yet the taste kept coming back to him, in spite of repeated cups of water that seemed to have little or no effect. Maybe the "C" rations would accomplish what the water failed to.

After looking at Dempsey and Franklin, Lt. Stracener knew in his own mind that they would be of little help again that day. They both appeared to be "death slightly warmed over." He thought at first he would mention it, but on second thought it was pretty obvious they were already suffering enough. He knew from past experience that Coast Guardsmen might fake some other kind of sickness from time to time to get out of work they didn't like. But faking sea sickness just wasn't done. There just wasn't any faking about these two fellows; all anyone had to do was look at them.

"I'll see if I can't get you guys transferred back to the WA-WA," Lt. Stracener said as he moved over to the compass to check the performance of the automatic pilot. They had nicknamed the contraption "Iron Mike" the day before after the problem of getting it disengaged at the take-off. The thing hadn't been working too well the day before and it was certainly not any better now from the look of things. For simplicity the crew had nicknamed the *Wachusett* the "WA-WA."

"Don't tell me they are going to start that again," Glass said, as one of the Japanese crew members came into the already crowded pilothouse with his hands extended out in front of him. He brought his feet together as though in leg irons, as the others had done, and then went through the "Mama San, Papa San, Baby San" bit, in the same singsong tone that so many before him had used.

"They're just looking for a little sympathy," Dempsey piped up.

"I believe they're coming for seconds," Glass replied as he looked over the intruder. He was positive that the fellow had made that same trip the day before. "I hope they aren't going to continue that procedure all through this trip. I just don't know if I can stand it."

Glass felt a little irritable that morning and certainly didn't believe there was room enough in the pilothouse for the entire boarding crew, as well as the Japanese crew going through their theatrics. Now would be a good time to get the hell out of there; he sure as heck didn't need any more of that right then.

As he left the pilothouse he debated whether he wanted to catch a little shut-eye right then or do a little more checking around the vessel. The thought of more sleep sounded too overpowering to pass up, so he headed back toward the roof of the cabin and his sleeping bag. He barely remembered the sleeping bag getting warm before sleep caught up with him.

There was no way of knowing how long he had slept until he glanced at his watch. The light was no brighter and the mist was as thick, if not thicker than it had been when he had lain down some two hours before. He did have to admit, though, that he felt better. Now if he could just find something to drink he would feel like a human being again.

He had gone through the ship before in search of spirits, but had done it in somewhat of a hurry. This time it was going to be different. He went about the search more systematically. He inspected every closet and cupboard, finding knives, guns, and all the other gear that would normally be carried on a fishing boat. There were plenty of Japanese cigarettes stored, but there just didn't seem to be anything that he wanted to take a chance on drinking. After all, one cough-syrup incident was enough.

The crew members he came in contact with during his search offered no objections to his inspection; they just stood by with wonderment on their faces. A couple of them showed surprise when he came upon their store of rifles, probably used for killing sharks or some such. Their surprise no doubt resulted from the fact that he made no move to take them. He merely looked them over and closed the cabinet again without so much as removing the ammunition that was also stored there. The whole thing just didn't make sense in their minds. If not guns, just what did he want? He would repeatedly make motions as though seeking a bottle to drink, but they knew they carried their own water aboard—why not anything else he might want to drink?

After a couple of hours searching, he gave the effort up as a bad job and headed back toward the bridge; at least the smell of fish wasn't as great there.

"What's new?" was his first comment after entering the pilothouse and noticing that there was a new batch of drawings on the blackboard. This time they seemed to be pointing up the nets. That part was obvious even to him.

"We're supposed to do our best to get them to tell us where their nets are," Lt. Stracener said.

"They still maintain that they didn't have any nets or fishing gear out when the chase started," Dempsey said, as he eyed Charlie and the captain.

"Have you tried that old bit about it won't cost them any more if they cooperate?" Glass asked, moving over next to the radio operator, as though to be buddy-buddy with him, and adding, "How're things, Charlie?"

Charlie looked around at Glass with a big grin and bowed a few times, but that was the extent of it.

The drawings and the attempted conversation went on for some time, the Japanese still insisting that they hadn't been fishing at all. Finally, with some more drawings and more conversation, a debate developed between Charlie and the captain. By the look on their faces it was not the happiest conversation that had ever occurred between them. The best the guardsmen could determine was that Charlie wanted to cooperate, but the captain wasn't at all sure it was a good idea, at least not at that time.

When the discussion appeared to be at its height, the fish company man appeared on the scene. He just seemed to appear out of nowhere and became an important part of the disagreement as soon as he arrived. The guardsmen just stood back and let the three of them go at it. They figured it was going to have to run its course. They only hoped that Charlie would be the winner when and if an agreement was ever reached.

The conversation went on for some time before apparently an agreement was reached. The captain and Charlie smiled at each other, then turned and bowed to the guardsmen as though they were asking, "What do you want now?" Yokoma exhibited his disgust by storming out of the pilothouse.

"I do believe they are trying to tell us something," Lt. Stracener said, looking over at Dempsey as though asking for another drawing that would get things moving again, or at least break the trance everyone seemed to be in. Dempsey grasped what the lieutenant was trying to say and moved over to the blackboard, pointing to the nets he had drawn before. He then went through the motions of pulling the nets in, hoping that would do the trick.

That seemed to do the job. Charlie turned to some of the radio equipment at the rear of the room and started pushing buttons as though he were dialing a push-button telephone, then turned and started bowing again.

It was only a matter of seconds when a beeping started. Charlie then moved over to the radio direction finder. With that, Glass's face lit up, "I think I have it. Apparently they have a homing device on their buoys and he has turned it on. Now all we have to do is home in on the beeps."

"I better let the Wa-Wa know what we have found," Lt. Stracener said, picking up the walkie-talkie.

After some conversation, to which Glass paid little or no attention, Lt. Stracener explained to the group that the *Wachusett* was real happy with their accomplishment and would pass the word on to the other vessels. After all, if one of the ships was going after its nets, the others would surely give up trying to hide the fact that they had nets out before the chase began.

Indicating that he meant Dempsey and Franklin, Lt. Stracener went on, "You fellows better get yourselves ready. The WA-WA is sending the whaleboat over with some more food and water for us, and you might just as well ride back with them when they get here." Neither needed further prodding; they had had their fill of the *Maru No. 8.* Away they went, heading for the door and on down to the deck. They had no intention of missing that whaleboat when it arrived.

"I'll go down with them," Glass said as he followed them out the door, "I'll have to unload the food and water they are bringing."

As they reached the deck, they could already see the whale-boat off in the distance. Apparently it had been in the water and waiting to leave before Lt. Stracener had talked with the *Wachusett*.

"I hope the food is something besides C Rations," Glass said as he took hold of the package one of the seamen passed him from the whaleboat when it pulled up alongside.

"I don't have the slightest idea what's in it," the seaman replied, "but you better have your feet braced because this container of water is heavier than hell."

Glass had to admit the seaman was right. The five-gallon container of water was heavy and a bit awkward to transfer from one boat to the other.

"I wonder how far away the nets are?" Glass asked when he had stowed the water and food in the corner of the pilothouse.

"As best I can determine from Charlie we aren't very apt to reach it before tomorrow at the very best. You have to remember they did one hell of a lot of running after they abandoned their nets."

"Yah, I guess you're right. According to the C-130's information, they were only about a hundred miles off Kodiak when they were seen fishing," Glass said, as he looked over Charlie's shoulder at some of the sophisticated radio equipment on the fishing boat. Then glancing back at Lt. Stracener he added, "Boy, they sure have some fancy gear on this tub. Look at it, fish finders, super modern fathometers, homing gear, transmitters, receivers, and that radar reaches out 40,000 yards. We should have gear like that on the WA-WA."

"Just think how they must have felt seeing us materialize out of the fog banks, knowing who we were and us getting bigger and bigger on their radar scope. I'll bet that must have really given them some kind of a thrill."

Glass thought a moment about it, then replied, "I guess you're right. Them knowing that we were coming to cart them off to some place where nightmares are made. That would be some thrill."

"Well, they must have known they were illegal," Lt. Stracener said. "If they didn't, they wouldn't have been running. They just didn't figure on getting caught."

"I don't think you're right about all that," Glass commented. "I doubt very much if the whole crew knew they were off base. I'll bet that the three I caught up here in the pilothouse were the only ones who knew where they were."

"You could be right," Stracener said, scratching his head. "These people don't let their right hand know what the left is doing most of the time." Then as he looked at the compass he added, "You know we are going to have to do something about this automatic pilot—darned thing keeps getting worse."

"Why don't I chase that radio operator down and see if they have any spare parts for the "Iron Mike" and then between the three of us we ought to be able to get that working better than it is anyway."

Lt. Stracener turned to him and said, "I think that's a good idea. If we are going to be steaming for a while to the net area, it would be a good thing to have it working right. We will certainly not reach the area tonight, if my guess is right."

Glass needed no further prodding. He was just as anxious to get the thing working as the lieutenant was.

19. STEERING PROBLEM

The light was just starting to fade as Glass returned to the bridge with Charlie and the captain. He likened the dimming light to that of a cocktail lounge when they lowered the lights to make it a little cozier. But why in the devil was he making that ridiculous comparison? Any imagined similarity between this place and a cozy cocktail lounge was absolutely ridiculous. With that he ushered the two Japanese into the pilothouse. He figured someone would have to steer the ship while the others worked on "Iron Mike." The captain had been picked for the steering chore.

"Our problem is that there is too much response when she veers off course a few degrees," Lt. Stracener said, as the front panel was removed from the automatic pilot.

"Maybe if some of these circuits were marked in English it would help," Glass replied and started poking around. "I sure can't figure out much from this diagram here on the panel." After they had laid the panel out on the top of the instrument and studied the drawing a while, Charlie moved up behind Glass and placed three new tubes by his hand. As he raised each one he pointed to a corresponding tube on the drawing, indicating that was where it should go.

"Let's give his idea a try," Stracener said as he picked up the first of the tubes and turned back toward "Iron Mike."

"I guess there isn't much else we can do," Glass commented as he took the other two tubes over along with the diagram. After the three tubes had been inserted in the places designated, they continued to study the diagram for a spell.

"I think I'm getting the gist of how this thing operates, and if I read it correctly, we should be replacing this tube as well," the Coast Guard officer said, pointing to another tube on the diagram. Charlie was looking over their shoulders, and when the tube was pointed to, he would just shake his head indicating that they did not have a replacement available.

"Well, I guess that does it. If they don't have one, we sure as hell are not going to replace it," Glass said.

"Let's give it a try with these new ones in it." With that, Stracener placed the panel back in position and replaced the screws that held it secure.

"It isn't as bad as it was," Glass said, after they had engaged the "Iron Mike" again and watched the compass to see what the result was.

"You're right. At least I think we can live with it now. I better call the skipper. He'll be happy to hear that we can steer now in a reasonably straight line." Lt. Stracener picked up the walkie-talkie and passed the information on in a blow-by-blow description, telling exactly what tubes had been replaced. He was just getting to the finale when a voice came back loud enough for even Glass to hear, "Ah, shut up and keep steaming!"

Lt. Stracener just stood there looking at the instrument, as though he couldn't believe what he had heard. When the realization had sunk in he gently laid the piece down as though, if it were to make a noise, it might offend the skipper on the other end.

To change the subject, Glass asked, "Do you want to take the first watch, or do you want me to?"

"If you don't mind, maybe it would be better if you did. I'd like to walk around the deck for a few minutes, then maybe I can get some sleep," was the answer, and with that the lieutenant slowly walked out of the pilothouse, leaving the other three to handle things.

It was shortly after Lt. Stracener left the bridge that the captain followed, knowing that Charlie and Glass had learned to get along, and he felt a little left out with the two. It just seemed at times that in spite of not being able to completely understand each other's language, those two were finding a way to communicate. He wasn't at all sure that he approved of the friendship, but for now there didn't seem to be a thing he could do about it. He had tried once.

With the wind and mist hitting him in the face as he paced up and down the deck, Lt. Stracener tried to get that "Aw, shut up and keep steaming" out of his mind. It just wasn't like the commander to talk to the other officers in that manner and he had figured the skipper had thought a little more of him than he had of the other officers. He had been given this chance for recognition, knowing that most of the other officers would have loved to have had the chance. It had not been his idea to burden the skipper by relating the details of the repair job. He merely thought that the commander would want to know that he and Glass were right on top of things on the fishing boat.

He knew in his own mind that he had been working hard for a good report from the commander when the proficiency papers were submitted to superiors. He had also figured that he was doing a better than average job in his present rank, and the possibility of becoming a lieutenant commander was his fondest hope. After all, hadn't it been him and the fellows with him that had broken down the Japanese to disclose where their nets were and how to home-in on them? None of the other boarding crews had been able to accomplish that. Sure, he had his heart set on moving up in the ranks, but wasn't that what every officer was after, at least those who intended to make the Coast Guard their career?

He knew that he would have to get this thing out of his mind if he was going to be able to sleep at all, and sleep he knew he had to have. In addition to relieving Glass on the bridge, tomorrow promised to be a big day. They should be coming on the nets, and there would be a great deal to do recording evidence when they did. He headed back to the bridge, convinced that he would forget the whole incident.

"Did the skipper call for me?" he asked as he entered the pilothouse.

"Nope, there hasn't been a peep out of anyone," Glass replied.

Lt. Stracener had no intention of discussing the matter with Glass. He didn't even want him to know that the incident was still bothering him.

As Glass moved back from where he had been standing beside Charlie, he bumped his head on the ceiling-light fixture, "Damn that thing. Why does it have to be so low?" he said with irritation, rubbing the top of his head.

"You're just a little too tall for this ship," the lieutenant said trying to surpress a smile. "I don't have any trouble with it." To prove his point he walked under it.

"Hell, I'm only about an inch taller than you," Glass remarked, as he removed his baseball-type cape and continued to rub his head. "I'll bet I've bumped that thing a million times already since coming aboard." Looking around at the lieutenant again, he added, "It's the difference in the color of the cap," referring to the fact that officers wore blue caps with an officer's insignia on the front while enlisted men wore colors depending on the division aboard ship they were assigned to. In the case of Glass, because he was assigned to deck division he was wearing orange with his rate displayed on the front.

"How's the 'Iron Mike' holding up?" the lieutenant asked, in a way of letting Glass know that he wasn't quite ready to retire for the night.

"Seems to be working a hell of a lot better than it did before, but I'd say there is still room for improvement." Glass leaned back against the bulkhead watching Charlie and the radar screen at the same time. "Where did you pick up all the moxie on electronics?"

"Well, I picked up most of it when I went through R.C.A. School, a few years ago," Stracener answered. "I have always been interested in the subject."

"You know, if we had the time we should take a look at their radar, at least this set out here," Glass said. Then moving over and laying his hand on the top of the set, he added, "It seems to get plenty warm at times."

"Gee, you know those radar sets can get pretty touchy, and without a good supply of replacement parts, we better just leave it alone until we have to do something about it," Stracener answered, as he moved forward and placed his hand on top of the set too. "Yes, I'll have to agree it is pretty warm." Then both men moved away from the set.

Glass leaned back against the bulkhead again. He knew that Lt. Stracener was up tight about something, but he didn't have any idea what it was that was troubling him. He had heard the skipper tell him to shut up, but he just couldn't believe that it had got to the lieutenant the way it had. He just leaned back waiting for him to open a new conversation if he was so inclined.

Lt. Stracener looked over at Charlie, then moved a step or two closer to Glass. "Have you noticed anything peculiar about that fish manager?" As he asked, he eyed Glass for a possible inkling of the reaction.

"Now that you mention it, yes," Glass replied. "He certainly seemed to stay at arm's length from me. But, by the same token I haven't been the least bit interested in making a friend of him."

"I don't mean that part," Lt. Stracener said. "I just noticed him keeping a close eye on me as I strolled the deck a few minutes ago. It certainly isn't the first time I have seen him sneaking around where I am."

"I haven't paid all that much attention to him," Glass commented, "but now that you mention it, he hasn't acted like he was enjoying the proceedings, to any degree. Those piercing eyes of his have a way of getting to me."

"I only brought the matter up, to remind you to keep your eyes open. I can't see what he hopes to accomplish by fighting us, but regardless of what the reason is, I think he bears watching," Lt. Stracener concluded.

During the many hours they had spent together on the fishing boat, they had gone into some detail on a great many subjects, including their children. Both had that in common—Lt. Stracener with two girls, and Glass with his one boy and another child due in a few months. They had talked some about the Coast Guard, and even electronics, but not too much about the lieutenant's favorite subject, religion. While Stracener took his religion quite seriously, Glass did not. The lieutenant rarely if ever took a drink of hard liquor, while Glass would drink almost anything, including cough syrup.

Glass didn't really object to discussing religion with him. He realized that the lieutenant would like to see him become a little more serious about it, but at least he wasn't continually trying to push it down his throat, like a great many others he knew. Maybe if the lieutenant had had a little more experience with drinking, he wouldn't have been so worried about Glass getting drunk on a couple of bottles of beer, like he had been the first day they were on the *Maru No. 8.*

Neither of the two guardsmen could recall how long they stood there silent. Each was more or less waiting for the other to reopen the conversation, and not in the least capable of figuring what subject to pursue.

It was Lt. Stracener who finally broke the ice with, "Say, how is that homing gear working? I don't suppose there is any way of telling exactly how far away the net buoys are?"

"I rather doubt that Charlie can tell exactly how far away they are, but I would judge that we have quite a way to go yet from the sound of the beeps," Glass answered.

"I don't suppose there is much chance of coming on them before daylight," Glass replied. "Didn't the skipper estimate that they were at least 150 miles away when we first started backtracking after the capture?"

"Yea, I guess you're right. We aren't making the best time in the world even though 'Iron Mike' is working better."

"I'll tell you one thing, this would be a lot easier for both of us if Dempsey and Franklin had been replaced, rather than the two of us being required to handle the whole job," Glass said, now hoping that the lieutenant would get going and get some sleep. Glass was already beginning to look forward to being relieved of the watch.

"Yes, it would have been better with two more men," Lt. Stracener said, adding, "Where in the world would they sleep?" He hadn't realized that Glass hadn't been made aware of a discussion he had held with Captain Forsterer earlier in the day. "I talked the matter over with the skipper, and we decided that because of the lack of accommodations here, Dempsey and Franklin are not going to be replaced. I think the two of us can handle the task."

Glass looked around at him, with surprise registered on his face. He had really believed that it would just be a matter of time and the two would be replaced, lightening the burden on the lieutenant and himself. "I suppose we can handle it all right, but for how long I don't know." Now there wasn't any question but that Glass mirrored his disappointment on his face.

Lt. Stracener stood around for a few more minutes. Then because there was nothing he could think of to ease the hurt that Glass was feeling from disappointment, he decided he had best get some shut-eye. He left the bridge without even saying goodnight or I'll see you later.

After he had left, Glass decided that he would make another attempt to get Charlie to produce something to drink. He tapped Charlie on the shoulder to get his attention. Then he went through the bit of taking a drink from an invisible bottle. As soon as Charlie saw him going through the motions, he gave a half bow and went into the back cabin. He hadn't been gone very long when he came back and handed Glass a decanter bottle. He waited until Glass had a chance to look at it, and then he burst out laughing. In spite of efforts not to, Glass couldn't help doing the same. Charlie had come up with another bottle of cough syrup.

After they had a good laugh, Glass set the bottle down untouched and just looked at Charlie, shaking his head back and forth. Charlie made motions as though he were looking over the radar and "Iron Mike," but he had a big grin on his face all the time he was doing it. It was apparent now to the Coastie that he might just as well forget getting anything to drink, at least on this watch.

Glass leaned back against the bulkhead again, watching Charlie check the wheel from time to time. He was learning to like this little Japanese and wished there was something he could do about the predicament that seemed certain to follow when they reached port. It was one of the few times during his years in the service that Glass actually wished he had made more of an effort to become an officer. He reasoned that had he more authority now he might be able to put in a good word for the man. He was still kicking such a thought around in his mind as Lt. Stracener entered the pilothouse.

"You ready for a few winks?" Stracener asked as he startled Glass out of his thoughts.

"Gee, you weren't off very long," Glass said. "What's the matter—thinking too much about pulling those nets tomorrow?"

"No, it isn't so much that as the fact that if we each take shorter watches tonight we will both be on hand the first thing in the morning," Lt. Stracener replied, adding, "I still have a funny feeling that we will be seeing them with the first light of dawn."

"You could be right," Glass answered. "I think I'm ready for a few minutes of shut-eye myself right now. Everything seems to be working all right." Then as he was clearing the door, "I'll see you after a bit."

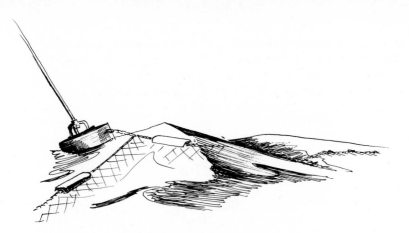

20. NET RETRIEVING

The custodians of the *Maru* 8 were both in the pilothouse listening to the beeps of the homing device as the sun put in an appearance the next morning. It was one of those mornings when it was hard to predict what type of weather they would be having in another two hours. For the moment the rays of the sun spread themselves out on the water like a warm blanket for several miles between them and a fog bank in the distance. The fog itself defied determining as to its direction of travel, density or depth.

While neither of them mentioned the fact out loud, both were hopeful the fog bank would evaporate long before they would be required to penetrate it. The two merely continued their vigil while chomping on a portion of "C" rations—something they both appeared to be doing more from habit now than desire.

They had barely finished what they termed as breakfast when Charlie came to life near the homing device. There was no doubt they were getting close to the first of the nets to be retrieved. The actual picking up of the gill nets was rather methodical. Glass and Lt. Stracener were intriguied as they watched the beginning from the pilothouse.

Only the Fish Manager remained in the pilothouse with them, and he appeared to resent the necessity of their nearness. The captain as well as the radio operator donned their foul-weather gear and headed for the deck of the ship to assist.

As the ship was swung around hard to starboard, Glass pointed to one of the net buoys they were pulling alongside. "I guess we have come upon them." The boat slid up close while one of the crew reached down with a boat hook and gently brought the buoy aboard. Both the ship handling and the recovery of the buoy were accomplished with obvious experience.

"Boy, they're treating that thing with kid gloves," Lt. Stracener remarked as he watched the buoy being disconnected from the beginning of the net that was now gradually coming on deck.

"I'd say they have a little money invested in those things. Probably worth their weight in gold," Glass said as he opened the door of the pilothouse. "As a matter of fact, I think I'll take a closer look."

As he headed down the ladder from the pilothouse, he noticed that Lt. Stracener was right at his heels. By the time they reached the rail the first of the net was already on board, and a lot of fish along with it.

Two fishermen were feeding the nets through two rubber roller winches that were situated about ten feet apart. The guardsmen had planned to move closer to the operation until they noticed about six of the fishermen were popping the fish, and what have you, out of the nets onto the deck. Both figured they had enough fish smell around them without having it on their clothes as well, so they retreated to a safe distance to watch.

Even as the first of the net came aboard, it was obvious that it was made of monofilament.

"Boy, this isn't going to help their case any," Lt. Stracener said, as he took a quick look and backed off again.

"That's forbidden for American fishermen, isn't it?"

"You better believe it is," Lt. Stracener replied with a scowl. "That stuff is a nonbiodegradable plastic material that never deteriorates, and if not retrieved would drift about the ocean continually killing fish and presenting a navigational hazard."

"Yah, we found out about that navigational hazard bit, not too long ago." Even as Glass said it he was thinking of only a week or so before when they had been sailing along the territorial water line in the Bering Sea. The *Wachusett* had torn into a group of nets set out to drift, and they didn't have the slightest idea by whom. What they did find out was that the nets completely fouled their prop, and until they put a diver over the side to clear it they were at the mercy of the sea. They had lucked out in several ways. It was fortunate they had the diver aboard, and in addition it provided the *Wachusett* crew with plenty of salmon to eat for a few days following the incident.

As he brought his mind back he commented, "Good gosh, you know after one of those nets fills up with dead fish it would sink to the bottom. Then when the seals and crabs got done eating all the fish out of it, the damned thing would come right back up and start fishing again. There just wouldn't be any end to it."

Lt. Stracener didn't even reply, merely shaking his head at the thought.

"Some of those nets appear to be around a mile long, with about a 4-1/2-inch mesh," the lieutenant said after a couple had been brought aboard. "We better make a note of that, and I had better get my camera and start taking some pictures of this operation. They will no doubt come in handy for the authorities when we reach Kodiak."

After the fish had been popped from the nets, the monofilament was fed into a tube when it had passed over rubber runners to the stern of the boat. There the nets were stacked and any remaining fish were removed. Lt. Stracener was now busy taking pictures as the fishermen worked. Both Coasties had to marvel at the lack of lost motion or duplication exhibited by the workmen.

Lt. Stracener brought out a package of labels, and as he handed them to Glass he said, "Why don't you label some of those nets so we can say positively they were the ones we saw being used?"

Glass accepted the labels and as he started fastening them remarked, "Boy, look at the variety of stuff coming in those nets!" He was referring to the seals, sharks, and birds, as well as a great many fish other than salmon.

"I'm not so concerned about the sharks and other stuff," Lt. Stracener answered, "but look at them, they're throwing away about 35 percent of the salmon, along with the other fish."

"Yah, I noticed that. They seem to be throwing away anything that isn't at least a foot and a half long, and on top of that even the big salmon are being chucked if they have a few marks on the head or gills. Really doesn't make much sense, does it? Unless, of course, they sell the cargo to a bunch of fish-head eaters." At the time he said it he fully intended to find out the answer the next time he and Charlie were alone.

"Looks like one heck of a waste of fish," the lieutenant chimed in, but what are they saving the sharks for? They don't seem to be throwing them overboard."

Above: This photo shows the production-line type of operation in the retrieving of nets by the Japanese fishermen. Below: Net buoys carried by the Japanese gillnet boats were equipped with the very latest in radio homing gear, thus giving the vessels little trouble in finding the buoys when they were ready to be retrieved. (Photos courtesy Lt. Cmdr. Robert H. Stracener)

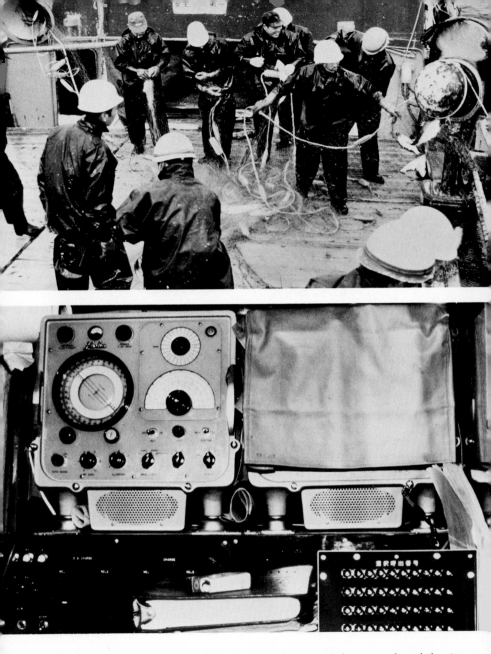

Above: Every crew member had his post when nets started coming aboard the *Jinmei Maru*. The monofilament nets carried more than just salmon. They had trapped seals, sharks, birds, etc. The Japanese would have abandoned their nets if they had been permitted to do so. Lower photo shows a small portion of the sophisticated electronic gear used for navigation and the homing device connected with their nets. (Photos courtesy Lt. Cmdr. Robert H. Stracener)

"Damned if I know," Glass answered, adding, "Didn't you say that was a 4-1/2-inch mesh on those nets? If I remember right, commercial gillnetters in the American waters are forced to use something like an 8-inch mesh. Now it just seems to me these Japanese nets aren't going to miss catching much that swims."

After what had appeared to be the last of the nets, the fishing boat continued to steam in circles for no apparent reason. The crew stood by making no effort to shift from their assigned posts. Movement seemed to come to a complete standstill as the ship continued to circle, until the Fish Manager stepped out of the pilothouse waving his arms and started jabbering away at the captain. The crew continued to hold their places as they looked to the captain for instructions.

"What the hell do you suppose that is all about?" Glass asked as he looked about for the radio operator and a possible explanation. After a few gestures proved ineffective, Glass and the radio operator headed for the pilothouse and the blackboard, with Lt. Stracener close at their heels.

"I'm beginning to feel like an old-maid schoolteacher," Glass said as he picked up the chalk and stood by the blackboard, "trying to get through to some stupid idiots." He knew by now that the Japanese wouldn't have the vaguest idea what he said.

"What do yo mean by the 'old-maid' schoolteacher?" the lieutenant asked, really looking puzzled.

"Well, I feel like an old maid or a nun; I'm sure as hell not getting any!" and with that Glass laughed more to himself than to anyone else. Lt. Stracener just ignored what he thought was a bad joke and motioned for Glass to get on with the pictures.

After a few drawings and a great many more gestures, it became apparent that one of the buoys was failing to answer the call for homing signals. The fishermen knew that the additional nets had to be in the area, but without the homing signal it was impossible to locate them. It was now obvious it wasn't something they were accustomed to, and they didn't seem to have any idea what to do about it.

"Well, there isn't much sense in hanging around here," Lt. Stracener said as he attempted to take command of the situation. "Those lousy nets could have sunk, or been picked up in the prop of some other boat. We better take what we have and head back for the *Wachusett* like they told us to."

The three climbed back to the deck where, after a few words from the captain, activity had already started, but this time of another sort. Everyone was turning to for the cleaning of the fish.

"There go your sharks overboard," Glass said, "but you notice they have cut off about six inches of the meat just above the tail. Come to think of it these people do eat a lot of shark stew. That must be the choice cut they are taking off."

"They sure have set themselves up into a real production line for the cleaning," Lt. Stracener commented between picture taking. "I would be willing to bet that some of our automobile manufacturers could take some pointers from them."

"I thought they were supposed to have copied everything from us," Glass answered as he swung around attempting to take in the whole scene.

A couple of the fishermen had equipped themselves with a combination knifehook that took the entire inner portion of the gill out of the salmon with one scoop. Each in turn passed the fish on to others who ran a knife up the full length of the underpart. The next group were equipped with a combination of spoon and knife, and again one sweep through the inside of the fish not only removed the innards but also the blood line that runs the length of salmon near the backbone. The efficiency and speed amazed both Glass and Stracener as they stood by in complete awe.

As the production line started, some of the deck boards were being removed by others of the crew, who picked them up and tossed them unconcerned into a pile. This surprised Glass as he watched. He had noticed the boards covering the cargo hold and the way they fit so tightly, appearing to have been worked over with a holystone to keep them looking so smooth. Now, seeing the men toss them around as though they had little or no importance had him wondering. They appeared to be about the size of a two-by-six-inch plank, standing on edge, but they showed so much wear on the top it was hard to tell what they had started out from.

He watched as a large section of them were moved, while at the same time some of the crew members were bringing out buckets of salt. Suddenly the whole thing made sense, as the fishermen started dobbing the salt on both the outside and inside of each fish. After they had been well salted, they were passed down into the hold where others stacked them like cordwood.

As soon as he realized what was happening, Lt. Stracener jumped down into the hold with his camera, and some more evidence shots were taken, without the least bit of interference from the crew. They went on with their work as though he didn't exist.

When the catch had been stowed and Lt. Stracener had completed his picture taking, the deck planks were replaced. It was then that Glass realized that the Japanese markings on the planks had a meaning. He noticed that they called for a certain plank as they progressed across the hold. Apparently the damned things were numbered and fit only in one particular spot—that was evidently how they get their tight fit. He was going to mention it to Lt. Stracener, but the lieutenant seemed preoccupied with his picture taking at the moment.

After the stowing had been completed, Glass noticed that the Japanese appeared to be in much better spirits. He couldn't put his finger on the exact reason, but assumed they felt better with most of their gear back, and the hold of the ship two-thirds full. They probably had far more to be happy about now than they had before. After all, they had run off and left their buoys and nets, certainly an investment that someone was going to have to be responsible for. Now, with the ship as close to full as it was, the crew was looking forward to a better pay-check on the return to Japan. Regardless of what their reasons were, Glass felt much relieved with the present atmosphere.

As he opened the door to the pilothouse, it became obvious that the *Wachusett* had been trying to get hold of them by walkie-talkie. Lt. Stracener had left the set in the pilothouse while taking the pictures and assisting with the labeling of the nets. Now it was fairly jumping up and down with beeping for someone to answer.

Glass picked the instrument up and acknowledged himself. When he heard Commander Forsterer's voice, "Where the hell you guys been?" he knew he didn't care to carry on any conversation and answered, "Just a minute and I'll get Lt. Stracener for you." With that he laid the walkie-talkie down and went back to the pilothouse door. He shouted down that the skipper wanted to talk to him and the lieutenant headed that way.

Glass didn't even want to be around for the ensuing conversation, so the two guardsmen passed on the ladder, each going in a different direction.

"This would be a hell of a good time to see if I can't find something to drink now that the crew seems to be in a fairly good mood," Glass said half out loud as he headed for the messroom of the ship. That, he figured, would be the logical place everything seemed to center around.

As he walked into the messroom he stopped short. Here a large part of the crew were gleefully tearing chunks of raw salmon and poking them into their mouths. He just couldn't believe it at first, but when he saw the radio operator standing with the others, he moved over to his side and watched a little closer. They would take a large chuck of seaweed and place in one cheek, then tear off a piece of the raw salmon, dip it in soy sauce, and pop that into the other cheek. The way they reacted after their mouth was full of the stuff, you would have sworn it was one of the better moments of their lives.

"Charlie," the radio operator, now quite sure of himself with Glass, kept nudging him to try the combination. With the amount of delight they seemed to be getting from it, Glass decided that it wasn't killing them, therefore it shouldn't kill him either. He decided that maybe a small portion would be enough for a start, so he moved in, took a small portion of the seaweed, and placed it in one cheek. The taste was similar to that of a mouthful of grass. Now with a small piece of the raw salmon dipped into the soy sauce in his other cheek, he started chewing as they were doing.

"Holy gad, what a miserable mess of shit," he said as he looked around for a place to spit out the concoction. There just wasn't any place to toss the stuff, and he just couldn't keep it in his mouth, so he swallowed. He didn't swallow just once; he had to continue swallowing because that mess didn't seem to want to lie quietly on his stomach. When he wiped the tears from his eyes and backed away in hope of not even having to smell it, he motioned for Charlie to come over.

"Now come on, Charlie," he said, "I just know that someone must have something to drink on this bucket of bolts." He then went through all the motions of tipping a bottle up and drinking. Charlie apparently got the message and after a great deal of discussion among those around the table, one of the fishermen took off running. A few minutes later back he came with a half-full bottle of Suntori.

With the vile taste of the seaweed and raw salmon still in his mouth, he was thrilled at the chance to tip the bottle up and swallow hard. He took three big drinks out of the bottle before he even offered to give it back. Both the owner and Charlie took a small swallow of the stuff and handed it back to Glass.

Now that Glass had the taste of the mess out of his mouth he remarked as he took another swallow, "This stuff tastes a great deal like our Scotch." It didn't take him very long to finish off the bottle.

Above: Two members of the Coast Guard boarding party view fish stowed aboard *Jinmei Maru 8*, after taking over vessel in illegal waters off coast of Alaska. Below: The hold, as it appeared to them, with stacks of select, illegally caught salmon. Salmon were cleaned, salted and then stacked like cordwood in the ship's hold. (Photos courtesy Lt. Cmdr. Robert H. Stracener)

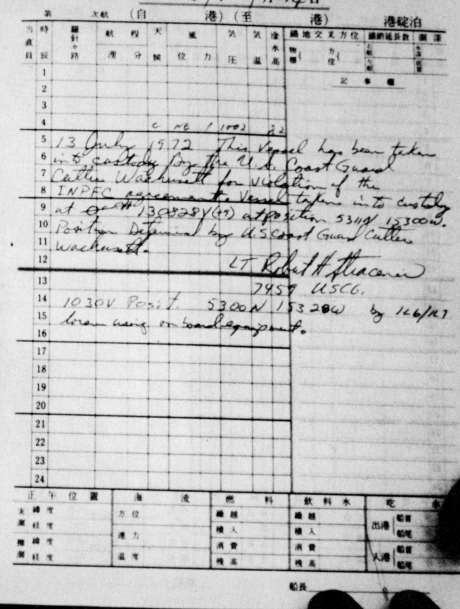

The Log-Book of the *Jinmei Maru 8* normally did not have entries made in English, but it did following the boarding by U.S. Coast Guardsmen on July 13, 1972: "This vessel has been taken into custody by the U.S. Coast Guard Cutter *Wachusett* for violation of the I.N.P.F.C. agreement." The location of the seizure was also entered into the log and signed by Lt. Robert H. Stracener. (Photo courtesy Lt. Cmdr. Robert H. Stracener)

A little more sign language with Charlie brought out the fact that each one of the fishing boats carried its own special commodity. *Maru No. 17* was carrying the bulk of the cigarettes for the fleet, while it was *Maru No. 19* that was carrying the liquor that might be needed on the trip.

"Wouldn't you believe it! I'm always on the wrong ship." Glass then decided he had better go back to the bridge and see how Lt. Stracener was making out with his talk to the *Wachusett*. Walking across the deck toward the pilothouse he began to feel a little glow and he knew the Scotch was taking effect. He just wished to hell that there was more of it to be had.

"Well, what's new?" he asked as he entered the pilothouse. He realized the minute he said it that Lt. Stracener was in no mood for jokes.

"The skipper must figure that we still have four men over here," Stracener shot back at him. "He seemed to think that at least one of us should have been with the walkie-talkie at all times. I sure can't carry that thing around with me every place I go."

Glass began to wonder if he had made a mistake coming back to the pilothouse. In an attempt to put the lieutenant in a better mood, he said, "Well, you have to admit he probably had his hands full catching and putting another crew on that second boat, then trying to get the nets all pulled."

21. RENDEZVOUS

The scene looked like the bargain basement of a woman's store with a sale in progress, as the *Citrus* and *Clover* completed the transfer of crews that had been aboard two of the Japanese fishing vessels. When the *Citrus* captain had completed the transfer of his crew members to replace those of the *Clover*, the latter was to go on with other patrol work. But now with the two buoy tenders, three Japanese fishing vessels, and the *Wachusett* milling in a circle around one another, it appeared to be pandemonium.

"Have you heard anything from Lt. Stracener's crew yet?" Captain Forsterer asked as he returned from the radio room where he had been listening in on the conversation between the two buoy tenders. It had become apparent the transfer was completed. Now it was the *Wachusett's* obligation to herd the four Japanese into Kodiak with an assist from the *Citrus*.

"Not a word. They apparently don't have anyone monitoring that walkie-talkie, or its out of commission," Lt. jg Holmes said as he looked around in hope of reading the captain's mood. He had thought previously that there had been a great deal of strain on him the last couple of days, and the captain hadn't been his usual cheery self as a result.

"Damn it, they were the first ones to head out for their nets. Can't figure what the hell can be keeping them, unless they are bringing those fish up one at a time," the captain said. Then as he paced back and forth a couple of times he added, "Keep trying to raise them, and let me know when you do."

Forsterer leaned against the starboard bulkhead debating with himself whether to continue to stand by with the other ships, who had already retrieved their nets, or go out in search of them. He knew in his own mind that it would be tricky now, with seven ships in the area, to find the exact pip on the radar that he was looking for. The weather was not good enough for the lookouts to identify anything more than 1000 yards away. In the matter of the recent Russian incident, there was always the chance that something had happened aboard the *Maru No. 8* that made it impossible for the guardsmen to get word out. If that were the case, he should be out there ready to lend a hand. How could he prove to his superiors that he had kept the *Maru 8* within even radar vision?

The more he thought about it the closer he came to a decision to give the order for a search. Right now he wouldn't have the additional aid of the *Clover*, but if the action wasn't taken soon, she would be on her way to resume her previous mission. It was not like Lt. Stracener not to report in. But, he did have to admit to himself that he had been rather gruff with the lieutenant the last couple of times he had reported about the trouble they had with the automatic pilot. Yet, that was still no reason to walk away without someone monitoring that walkie-talkie.

Well, he would give them just five more minutes and if he hadn't heard anything by then, he'd find them, and if they were in good shape, woe be unto that lieutenant! To keep his mind off the point, he started to compliment himself on the fact that he had seen to it that the prize crews from the *Burton Island* and *Clover* had been exchanged the day before, and the *Citrus* men had successfully completed their transfer of personnel. The *Burton Island* had pressing business in the Bering Sea and should not be detained any longer than necessary. The radio had informed the Coast Guard ships that the *Clover* was to resume original patrol orders as soon as possible. The more he thought about the *Clover* leaving the scene the more he was concerned about one of the radar pips leaving his screen. As long as six pips remained, he felt he was safe, but on the other hand, was he?

He had been given the responsibility, along with the *Citrus*, of getting these fishing boats on into Kodiak, but with this damned fog it was pretty hard to figure out what anyone else was doing.

The lieutenant broke into his thoughts with, "I've got them." Captain Forsterer accepted the walkie-talkie that was being offered. He started talking into it, and as he did he walked out onto the port wing where the conversation would not be picked up by the other officers on the bridge. When he returned to the pilothouse he seemed a little happer with himself as he laid the instrument back down in front of the lieutenant.

He handed the drawing of where each ship was to position itself for the convoy sailing to the lieutenant, saying, "See if you can't get them into place as soon as the *Maru No.* 8 gets here. Then maybe we can be on our way to Kodiak."

The captain then moved back where he could keep an eye on the radar scope and still be sure to have a pretty good idea of what was taking place on the bridge. It was going to be his duty to fill out a fitness report on the other officers under his command, and this would be a good test for Lt. jg Holmes.

As he eyed the back of the lieutenant, he wondered just what kind of fellow he really was. The guy seemed to do his job fine, but he was really difficult to get to know. He seemed to prefer to spend his time reading rather than entering into the fishing and card playing with the other officers. Pretty hard to figure out exactly what he did want out of life. Of course, if it wasn't for the fact that their private life did affect their performance, it would be none of his damned business.

"*Citrus*, this is the *Wachusett*. Why don't you take off now, slowly, and try to keep your two prize crews in line as much as you can as I described to you," Lt. Holmes was saying into the walkie-talkie. "You had better take it pretty easy to start. We have one more of our people to pick up yet." With that, he turned to the radarman, adding, "I will want a close watch on that screen, and let me know if any of the vessels start getting to close together."

"Aye, aye," was the only answer he received as the radarman devoted all his attention to the screen in front of him.

The convoy pattern the captain had laid out called for the *Citrus* to take the point. Then the two fishing vessels with their crew members aboard were to cruise alongside each other 1000 yards astern of the *Citrus*, maintaining a distance of 2000 yards apart. The *Wachusett* would bring up the rear at a distance of 1000 yards. Lt. Holmes was telling himself at the time—This all looks real good on paper, but trying to teach fishermen how to steam in a military convoy pattern was going to be something else. Holmes realized that the skipper was handing him a hot potato with this assignment, but he was going to do his level best to make things work out right.

"Sir, I believe this one pip is the *Maru No. 8* moving into position," the radarman said after a few minutes.

"Fine," Lt. Holmes said as he picked up the walkie-talkie and depressed the communicator button, "Lt. Stracener?" Apparently there was an acknowledgement from the other end. He went on, "Take up a course of 45 degrees from where you now are. You will have the *Maru No. 18* on your starboard. Try to keep at least 2000 yards between you. The *Maru 23* will be in front of you, and try to keep 1000 yards astern of them. We will be maintaining a distance of 1000 yards astern of you, but you won't have to worry about us. We'll be keeping an eye on you." With that, the lieutenant laid the instrument down and again turned to the radarman, "Did you get the positions I described?"

"Aye, aye. The *Maru 8* is moving into position now and picking up the correct course," the radarman answered.

"That's fine. Now if you get the least bit tired, call for some relief," Lt. Holmes said, adding, "I sure don't want anyone running into each other in this snotty weather. I'll be depending on you."

The *Wachusett* had been lying dead in the water waiting for the balance of the ships to get into the convoy position they would be steaming. Now that everyone had started moving away from them, Lt. Holmes passed the word for "Forward one-third speed." He figured he would let them get a bit ahead and that way he could get a better idea of what kind of cruising speed they were going to be able to maintain.

After a few minutes of steaming at one-third speed, Lt. Holmes looked at his watch, then at the radarman, "I want to be kept informed if we drop back too far. I want to try to keep within 1000 yards of them."

"We're just about that behind the *Maru 8*, but *Maru 18* has moved out. Apparently she is keeping up with the ships ahead because they have moved away considerably."

With that information Lt. Holmes again picked up the walkie-talkie, "*Maru 8?* What seems to be the problem? You're letting everyone else run away from you!" Then after a short pause he said, "You mean that's the best speed that you have?" again talking into the instrument.

Lt. Holmes seemed to be mulling the answer over for a few seconds before he again talked into it, "*Citrus?* I guess that you are going to have to cut your speed a little. Our *Maru 8* can't maintain present speed you're making." After enough time to have received an answer he again set the walkie-talkie down in front of himself.

"That *Maru 8* could probably make better speed if they didn't wander back and forth as much as they do," the radar-man said, almost expecting the lieutenant to tell him what was wrong.

"*Maru 8?* This is WA-WA again. Are you having some kind of steering problem? You seem to be wandering a lot back and forth. Try to steer in a straight line on the 45-degree bearing." Holmes peered from a spot behind one of the windshield wipers hoping to be able to see the ship that had to be a few hundred yards in front of them. Then without looking at anyone in particular, he said, "They're having more automatic pilot problems, and say that is the best they can do unless they disconnect it and steer by manual means."

Things continued rather quietly on the bridge of the *Wachusett* for close to an hour before Commander Forsterer moved forward and picked up the walkie-talkie. "*Maru 8*, this is the captain. You drifted over to within 500 yards of the *Maru 18* on that last swing to port. Maybe you better disengage that damned automatic pilot if it can't do better. I sure as hell don't want you ramming them on one of your swings." He then turned to the radarman, "You're supposed to inform the O.O.D. before things get to the point that they just were. There could have been an accident before anyone was aware of what was happening. How in the hell did you know but what they had all gone to sleep on that *Maru 8?*"

Lt. Holmes just stood dumbfounded. He had no way of knowing what was taking place until it was all over. He was still trying to think of something to say when the radarman replied, "I figured if they were having automatic pilot problems, the ship would correct itself in time."

"Yes, and you also know from watching that screen that their veering was getting worse by the minute, and if they hadn't disconnected it they would have been all over the ocean in a few more minutes," Captain Forsterer shot back at him. Then added, "If you need some help on that screen, say so like the lieutenant said. But I do want the Officer-of-the-Day to know what's going on so he can take necessary action, and take it in time."

Forsterer's face softened as he stepped over to Lt. Holmes, gave him a little pat on the shoulder, and said, "Things seem to be going fine here so I think I'll turn in for a little sack time. Don't feel bad about calling me if you need anything," and with that, he turned and left the bridge.

Lt. Holmes felt pretty good that the captain had not seen fit to give him some type of reprimand along with the radarman. After all, it was the duty of the Officer-of-the-Day to know exactly what was going on at all times when he was in charge.

When he was sure that the captain had left and was out of earshot, he turned to the radarman saying, "Why don't you get some help to spell you on that screen? This is going to be a long watch, and I'm going to have to know what's going on, like the captain said." Then, thinking for a minute, he asked, "Is your department short handed because of the prize crews?"

"No, sir," the radarman replied, "Dempsey came back from the *Maru 8* because he couldn't take the roll of that ship. We could call him."

"That's fine," Holmes said, then turning to the messenger on duty, "Why don't you roust Dempsey out to help on this watch?" With that he felt he had salved the wound a little with the radarman. Before the messenger could clear the bridge, he added, "Say, you could bring us up a couple of pots of coffee. I don't think it'll hurt anyone."

As the lieutenant looked out the front window he thought he saw a faint flicker of light. He quickly moved out on the port wing. He couldn't see how in this kind of weather he could see the *Maru 8*, even though she was only supposed to be 1000 yards ahead of them. As he made a grab for the railing to hold his balance, he was sure that occasionally there was a light up ahead, slightly to starboard. There was no doubt of it now, because the fog had lifted somewhat and the *Maru 8* could be seen from time to time. "Let me know if she moves very far out of line," he said to the lookout as he retreated back to the shelter of the pilothouse.

The messenger had already returned with the coffee, and as Holmes entered, a cup of the steaming brew was passed to him. He hadn't realized how much he had chilled in the short space of time he had been on the wing, but the cup of coffee tasted even better than he had hoped it would at the time he had requested it.

"Things should be a bit easier now with the fog lifting," he said. He wasn't talking to anyone in particular, but the sound of his own voice seemed a little reassuring. He just hoped the balance of this watch would go as smoothly as it was now. The only present trouble was in trying to get a little more speed out of *Maru* 8, but as far as he was concerned let someone else handle that chore on the next watch. He just wanted them to keep their place in the convoy formation.

Lt. Holmes looked over at the two radarmen, wondering now if he had done the right thing in calling Dempsey to duty. Should the fog clear completely, they would be far less dependent on the radar to see that the two *Marus* ahead of them stayed on their stations. Maybe he had better consider relieving one of them if the fog did not worsen in the next few minutes. There wouldn't be any point in having two men on that station.

It was while Lt. Holmes was debating with himself on the advisability of having two radarmen on duty, that one of them, Dempsey, said, "Sir, we seem to be drifting more and more to starboard in relation to *Maru* 8 and *18.*"

Lt. Holmes walked over to the screen, and after a short watch one of the pips identifying the two ships, he approached the helmsman, "Have you been sticking to that 45-degree heading?"

"Yes, sir, as much as possible," the young seaman replied, "but it is a little difficult to hold her in an exact straight line."

"Ease her over to port a bit," Holmes said. Then noticing that the light on the stern of the *Maru* 8 was visible a good deal of the time now, he pointed it out to the helmsman and said, "Try to hold the *Maru* 8 on the starboard bow, with that 45-degree heading and we'll be all right."

The sky was just beginning to turn gray as Lt. jg Jones came on the bridge with, "Well, are your ready for some relief, Lt. Holmes?"

"You bet I am," was the reply. "This job makes you feel like a sheep dog with a flock of idiot lambs." He explained the heading they were attempting to maintain, then excused himself and headed for the wardroom for some food. Next, he would be ready to catch a few hours of shut-eye, which he felt was well earned.

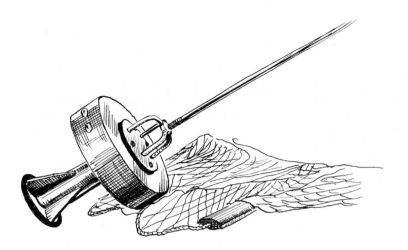

22. "CONVOY"

Even though the watch officer aboard the *Wachusett* believed he had his troubles with the *Maru No. 8*, they did not begin to compare with the problem the two Coast Guardsmen were having aboard that Japanese vessel. Lt. Stracener was still on the bridge with the Fish Company Manager Yokoma, standing over the wheel watching the performance of the "Iron Mike" when the call from the WA-WA came in.

"Yes sir," Lt. Stracener was saying into the walkie-talkie, "We are having a heck of a lot of trouble with the automatic pilot. Aye, aye, sir, yes, we will switch to manual steering if we are getting that far off course."

Even as Glass heard the lieutenant agree to change over to manual steering, he knew that this was going to prove to be a long night. It would naturally be his job to spell whoever the Japanese had on the wheel. Right now it was that damned Fish Manager. Glass and he had never hit it off like he did with Charlie, but he guessed that he was going to have to live with it.

Lt. Stracener made motions that he wanted the "Iron Mike" disengaged to the Fish Manager, then indicated on the compass that he wanted a course of 45 degrees steered. After the fishing boat was on course, he stepped back and watched for a couple of minutes. When he was content that things were going as well as could be expected, he merely nodded to Glass and said, "Well, see you in a few hours," and away he went.

Glass stood back, just letting his eyes roam from the radar screen to the Fish Manager's back as he stood at the wheel. It had been in his mind just to let the guy stand there and steer the vessel as long as he would without relief. He figured the fellow didn't merit a great deal of cooperation; he certainly hadn't granted much, but after close to two hours had gone by he decided better. He moved up in back of the Japanese, indicating that he would take the wheel. There was no objection. As a matter of fact, the fellow seemed quite relieved to have the chance to stretch and rest his eyes.

Even as Yokoma stepped back from the wheel, he knew that with his military background he would rather have stood at the wheel until he dropped from exhaustion than to have given in and asked for relief. The fact that the young guardsman had taken over the wheel did not change his opinion of them or what they were doing to his career. They would never get his respect, and he wouldn't be afraid to tell them so at the proper time.

After Glass had moved up closer to the windshield he noticed that the fog had cleared a great deal, and he could see the light of the fishing boat, supposedly 1000 yards ahead, that they were following. Good, he told himself, that should make the going easier. Now all he had to do was keep an eye on the radar screen enough to make sure they stayed the 2000 yards to starboard of the *Maru 18*.

As he watched the compass and swung the wheel first one way and then the other, holding the ship as close to the 45 degrees as he could, he felt the presence of the Fish Manager beside him. He looked over as he was reaching up to the radar set slightly above their heads. The Japanese placed his hand on the set, then quickly jerked it away, shaking his hand as though it had been burned.

Now that Glass thought about it he had noticed that there was an awful lot of heat coming from it—a whole lot more than there should have been if the set were working right. Apparently whatever was wrong with it was not affecting the screen any because it was putting the pips where they should be, judging from the fishing vessel they could see up in front.

Glass made no objections when the Japanese reached up and turned the set off. He figured there was still the set in the room behind the pilothouse if he felt he really needed to look at it occasionally. With the weather as clear as it was, he could concentrate on following directly behind the fishing boat in front.

After an hour or so Glass found that he was forced to strain his eyes more and more to see the light in front. On occasion the light was lost to him, and he knew that it had to be the result of an inconsiderate fog bank getting in their path. After a few trips to the back room to check position, he decided that was just too much running. He reached up and switched the master radar set back on. As far as he was concerned it was just too much trouble to run into the radio room and check that repeater set.

It hadn't been on very long when the Fish Manager again reached up and laid a hand on the set. Again he jerked it off as though he had been burned. When he reached up again, he shut the set off. "Look, boy," Glass said, "Buddha will take it in the butt before I try to steer this tub without that set." It wasn't as much what Glass had said that caused the Fish Manager to back up as the tone of voice when he said it. The set stayed on, and although it continued to put out a great deal of heat it worked fine.

Glass was glad to have Charlie show up on the bridge. It was evident that Charlie was relief for the Fish Manager. The two barely acknowledged each other as one came in and the other left. Glass was glad to turn the wheel over to Charlie. Before stepping back he nodded toward the master radar set, hoping that the radio man might have some kind of solution to the problem.

Charlie reached up, put his hand on the set, then shrugged his shoulders as though to say, "Ah, let it burn up if it wants to."

Glass sure as heck had no intention of trying to steer the ship without that set, and he was sure in his mind that Charlie didn't either. The more Glass thought about it the more he wanted the set on. They had already caught hell once from the WA-WA for wandering off course. Why should they push their luck now?

As the horizon started lighting up, Glass watched Charlie a little closer than he had been. It was clear the guy was in a better mood than he had seen him since the cough syrup incident. He figured that something was up when Lt. Stracener put in his appearance, and the Japanese turned the wheel over, pantomiming he needed to go to the restroom.

Glass took the wheel, thus allowing Lt. Stracener to get the feel of the situation, before completely turning the ship over. He had just finished telling the lieutenant about the master radar set when Charlie came back in with the fishing boat captain. The captain immediately took over the wheel from Glass and indicated that Charlie wanted him to follow. With a puzzled look, Glass followed him out of the pilothouse and down across the deck toward the mess room.

There were several Japanese fishermen in the room when they entered, and to Glass's surprise one of the Japanese greeted him with "Good morning." When the immediate shock wore off, Glass asked where the fellow had been keeping himself, especially when they were trying to get through on the first and second day of the boarding.

Even though the Japanese was a little rusty on some English words, Glass was able to decipher that the Fish Manager had been responsible for the English-speaking fisherman staying hidden until now. Even at this point it had been over the argument of the captain and Charlie that Glass was being allowed to talk to him. He had the feeling all along that there was something he didn't like about that Fish Manager, and now he had good reason for that feeling.

"You aren't going to try to tell me that you never saw an airplane, are you?" Glass asked.

"No, we see many," the Japanese said, and swooped his arms indicating how some came right down to the wave tops. In the description of the helicopter the Japanese indicated that the aircraft had nearly landed on their deck. Even the interpreter was described in detail. Glass just shook his head in disbelief.

"Why in the world did you guys try to run?" he asked.

"Fish man want, we run," was the answer.

After nearly an hour of chatting with the man, while Charlie stood by, occasionally feeding some new ideas for the man to convey to Glass, the conversation seemed to lag. Most of the questions the crew and Charlie had been feeding the fisherman to be passed on to Glass involved where they were being taken, and how long they would be held.

At first, Glass tried to point out that he had no idea of how long they would be held. He did tell them, however, that it was to Kodiak that they were being taken, and that he felt sure that if they continued to cooperate as they had been it would only be a short time that they would be held. He didn't even attempt to answer their questions in regard to how much fine they would be expected to pay, or if there even would be a fine, but again assured them that coopertion was the keynote and could have a great deal to do with what the outcome was.

Both the crew and Charlie seemed to be satisfied with the answers that he had given and they eased off on questions for which he had no answers. The long watch had taken its toll on

Glass. He started moving toward the door, and, he hoped eventually, toward his sleeping bag. He made a gesture with his hands and his head that he wanted to get some sleep. With a few Japanese words from Charlie, the crew bowed several times and permitted him to leave the mess hall.

Heading out, he began to sympathize with the fishermen. As he thought of it, the average Japanese spent his life going to sea; his livelihood depended on his catch, and the U.S. agreement with Japan meant very little to him. In the Japanese mind it meant an invisible line far enough away from land that, for all appearances, left him still in the middle of the ocean even after crossing it. How do you say the fish on the left side of a whitecape are yours, and all that are on the right side belong to us? Yes, he could see why the Japanese fishermen could be confused, and one of the reasons they seemed a bit hostile when the Coasties first came aboard.

Even after he snuggled into the sleeping bag he felt a little sorry for the fishermen. Oh, he didn't feel the least bit concerned about people like the Fish Manager, who no doubt had a great deal to do with the invasion. But the way he saw it, the fishermen would be tied up in Kodiak for some time until the whole mess was cleared up, and it wouldn't be just the Fish Manager who would be suffering. Without work, the families of the fishermen could well suffer, and it would really have been none of their doing. It was only because he was so tired that the subject left his mind and sleep caught up with him.

It was close to noon before Glass climbed out of the sleeping bag and headed for the pilothouse, where he hoped to find some "C" rations and at least a drink of water. He related part of the events to Lt. Stracener when he reached the bridge, but at the moment, the lieutenant seemed to be preoccupied with thoughts of his own. The officer indicated that it wouldn't be necessary to relieve him for a while yet, so he took his leave and headed back toward the deck.

The feeling for the Japanese fishermen weighed heavily on his mind for a time, but realizing that there was little or nothing that he could do about the situation, he did his best to get his mind on other things.

Wandering around on a ship as small as the *Maru 8* can get quite boring after a couple of days and Glass was finding that out. It wouldn't have been nearly so bad if there had been a little to drink, or even if there had been someone that he could talk with besides Lt. Stracener. As he continued to search for something to occupy his time, he dearly wished for the library aboard the *Wachusett.* He remembered setting the library up shortly after going aboard the cutter in November, 1970. On finding so much off-duty time on his hands, he couldn't figure why no one had ever set one up before. He certainly had made every effort to get one. By gaining permission to use $50 out of the Morale Fund, and the assurance of $50 additional after each patrol, the project had got under way. He had then set out to find a book store that would give him some type of co-operation. After considerable checking in the Seattle area, and letting store owners know what his problem was, results had started to materialize. Some merchants had offered half price, while there were still others who made outright donations to the effort. The *Wachusett* now had a fairly complete library with approximately 900 books, all current. True, a great many of the books were only paperbacks, and some were even without covers, but they covered a great many subjects.

Yep, the *Wachusett* had a library but it sure wasn't doing him one bit of good right now. There were some books on the *Maru 8;* he had seen them when he searched the vessel, but they offered little for him besides the chance to look at a few pictures.

He realized after a bit that it wasn't going to help one bit to walk around patting himself on the back for starting the library. While he knew, deep down, that he had put in a lot of work getting the thing started, he had also received a great deal of satisfaction in having the books he wanted when he wanted them—but no amount of wishing was going to bring the library to him now.

Heading back toward the bridge with the idea of relieving, he encountered the English-speaking fisherman on deck, apparently getting as much daylight as possible now that his seclusion was over. Glass debated whether he wanted to join in conversation with him or not. He certainly didn't want to discuss possible fines or confinement. The thought weighed too heavily on his mind from the last encounter.

The Japanese fisherman, who had no intention of renewing the conversation either, pointed to the *Wachusett* and inquired as to its speed. "Your ship, eight knots," Glass said, pointing to him and the *Maru 8*, then adding, "My ship 34 knots." This seemed to impress the Japanese very much. Glass had to feel a little guilty after saying what he had. He knew that going downhill, the very best the *Wachusett* could do was about 18 knots, and if it were to drop from the top of the Empire State Building it might get up to 34 knots before hitting the ground.

They hadn't much more than started their conversation when a Coast Guard helicopter came hovering over the fleet, first crowding close to one fishing vessel and then another. When it moved in close to the *Maru 8*, the Japanese fisherman disappeared with fear in his face as though he expected that they might be dropping bombs.

Glass decided that it was time to return to the pilothouse; just possibly Lt. Stracener would know what this all meant.

"We're already getting a reception," Lt. Stracener said as soon as Glass had closed the door to the pilothouse.

"What's it all mean?" Glass asked.

"Oh, I guess it is some of the big wheels from the National Fisheries coming out to see how the convoy is progressing, and it wouldn't surprise me if they haven't taken a few pictures. You know it's only going to be a couple more hours and we will be pulling into Kodiak. They should be passing the word pretty soon as to just where we will be docking."

"That's just jolly with me," Glass commented.

Lt. Stracener turned and looked at Glass saying, "What's the matter, are you getting a little tired of "C" rations?"

"You just better believe I am," Glass answered. "I just can't wait to get a good meal under my belt."

"Well, you can relax because we should be tied up in time to have good chow on board the cutter tonight," the lieutenant commented.

"I'll tell you it is really going to feel good to get off this tub. I'm beginning to have the feeling that I have spent about half my life on here already," Glass remarked.

"I have to agree with you it does seem like we've been on here close to a lifetime, and I'll be glad when it is over myself," Lt. Stracener agreed.

When land came into view, more and more aircraft from Kodiak sailed close overhead, and as the activity increased it became obvious to both Coast Guardsmen that the Fish Manager, Charlie and the captain were becoming jittery. It had to be their fear of the unknown, Glass reasoned as he watched them nervously going about the duties of preparing the ship for tying up to a dock that was as yet unseen.

The Fish Manager moved over to take charge of the wheel and it became apparent to the two Coast Guardsmen that he would be the one handling the actual docking. This had little meaning for them except that they knew they did not want any part of the actual maneuvering. The close call with the *Wachusett* on the first boarding had been about all the ship handling, in close quarters, that either of them cared for.

23. NO GREETING

Woman's Bay was alive with newspaper writers, photographers, National Marine Fisheries Service personnel and Coast Guard officials as the four fishing boats pulled into port followed by the *Wachusett.* The *Citrus* was maneuvering in the background, waiting until the others were located before moving into position.

The *Maru No. 8* was the last of the fleet to be tied up, being the slowest vessel; it had held the convoy back from the very beginning. Now it appeared she would have been swamped with curiosity seekers had there not been security lines put up to hold the mob back. But even with that, there were flash-bulbs popping and complete confusion nearly everywhere.

Both Glass and Lt. Stracener sighed with relief as the *Maru 8* was made secure to the inboard fishing boat. Now all that remained for them was to be officially relieved of the responsibility of the ship. Lt. Stracener had been told that the National Marine Fisheries would accept that responsibility when the boats were tied up at Kodiak, but for the moment everyone looked like an official and no one came forward with a reprieve for them. The two just looked at each other, hoping the other would come up with a suggestion.

After what seemed like hours of waiting, Lt. Stracener picked up the walkie-talkie and called several times before receiving any response. Then after a brief conversation with the *Wachusett*, he turned to Glass, "If you'll just stand by for a little bit I'll go sign whatever papers have to be signed, then we can be on our way."

Glass watched the lieutenant disappear through the crowd, then motioned for the captain and Charlie to relax, as they looked over to where he was leaning against the bulkhead. It seemed logical that they should turn to him for instructions. It was also a real concern to Glass as to what was expected of him, let alone what he was supposed to tell them. He would have liked nothing better than to be relieved so that he could go back to the cutter for a warm shower and a square meal.

Because they were not next to the dock there was less commotion real near, and because of that he envied the Coasties on the *Maru 19*, now moored on the *8's* port side. Being closest to the dock there was a good chance they would be relieved of their responsibility before he would. As he kicked the thought around in his mind he glanced in their direction.

As he looked, he noticed that Gunner's Mate "Moose" was being assisted to the dock by two of his shipmates. As he continued to watch, he figured that "being assisted" might not be the words he wanted to associate with the affair as the two were doing more carrying than anything else. Now this was something rare. The six-foot-three-inch, 280-pound Coastie seldom needed assistance in doing almost anyting he set his mind to, but there it was right before his eyes. At first Glass was going to walk over and ask what the problem was; certainly "Moose" hadn't been seasick. He probably just fell or was injured in some way while on the fishing boat. Assuming that their boat rolled and tossed the same as the *Maru 8* had, there was every chance in the world that "Moose" could have lost his balance and hurt himself. The pair helping "Moose" didn't appear to be too concerned about what they were doing, and in a few minutes he would see them back on the Wa-Wa anyway. Right then he was thinking how soon he would be relieved himself.

Even though he might have shouted over for an explanation, he was interrupted by what appeared to be a fisheries official heading his way. He just stood pat, hoping against hope that was who it was, and looking the fellow over.

The man was shorter than Glass. He looked to be about five feet six and was wearing heavy hornrimmed glasses. There didn't appear to be much question but that he was unsure of himself, as he delicately picked his way around some of the fishing gear that was scattered about the deck.

"Stop those fishermen from talking to one another," was the first comment the fisheries man made when he got within earshot of Glass. As Glass looked to where he was pointing, he noticed that after the two fishing boats had been tied side-by-side, the Japanese crews seemed to be exchanging stories. No doubt they were telling the experiences they had encountered after being seized by the Coast Guard.

After reviewing the reunion for a few seconds, Glass turned back to the fisheries man and said, "Go to hell!" After a couple of minutes of looking at Glass in disbelief, the official stormed off, not in the direction of the conversing fishermen but toward the bridge of the *Maru 8*.

Glass interpreted this move to be his relief, and with that he waved to Charlie and the captain and headed for the dock and a chance to get back aboard the cutter, now tied up several yards behind the fleet.

"What in hell are you doing here?" Glass asked as he noticed that Seaman Kelly was standing around looking as though he were lost.

"I was looking for you," the seaman replied. "I just wondered if you were all right. I couldn't figure out which of these boats you were on after I got down here."

"Oh, I get it, now you were just worried about whether I lost your knife of not," said Glass smiling.

"Hell, you can keep the knife if you want to. I didn't see you come back to the cutter when the rest of the fellows did and I wondered if you were okay," he said, now a little apologetic at having braved the crowd.

"Take it easy, kid," Glass said, then added, "Say, how would you like for me to give you a tour of a Japanese fishing boat?" and with that he couldn't help laughing.

"Will you be serious?" Kelly put in. "Some of the guys are going into town to some floating joint, and I wondered if you wanted to come along."

"Naw, leave me out of anything tonight," Glass replied. "I'm going to get something to eat, a good shower, and then hit the sack. Thanks anyway." Glass walked down the dock with the young seaman, and wished him a good time as the two parted near the gangway of the *Wachusett*.

As he exchanged salutes with the deck officer he turned to watch his reaction. Not realizing that Glass was observing him, the officer had pinched his nose with his thumb and index finger, indicating a bad odor originating from the crewman.

Hell, Glass thought, what could the guy expect from someone who had spent three days and nights on a Japanese fishing boat without benefit of clean clothes or a shower? Knowing that it wasn't only his underarm deodorant that had failed him, he headed straight for his locker, clean clothes and a refreshing shower. He would have enjoyed spending a couple hours soaking in a hot bathtub but that was out of the question aboard a Coast Guard cutter.

He was just a few minutes behind the prize crew from the *Maru 19* when he entered the mess hall of the cutter. He had visions of a nice, thick steak, mashed potatoes, and the other fineries that go with it. He really believed that after better than three days of "C" rations there would be no question but that orders would be passed for the cook to round up a hearty meal for the members of the prize crews.

"I've been keeping it warm for you guys," the cook said as he motioned for them to hurry up and eat so things could be washed and put away. It was apparent they were to eat the same fare the rest of the crew had had for an evening meal.

Reluctantly Glass scooped up a batch of the spaghetti, covered it with some meat sauce, and headed for one of the mess tables. Two of the *Maru 19* members were sitting across from him merely picking at the chow. Disgust was written all over their faces.

"What's the matter, not hungry?" Glass asked as he moved his plate over in front of himself.

He didn't receive an answer, so stuffed his mouth full of the mess he had on his plate. Then he looked up and even though they hadn't said a word, he remarked, "I see what you mean. This damned stuff is not only cold but wasn't worth a s--- when it was hot," and with that he just let his fork drop on the table.

"To hell with this crap," one of the others said, "let's go downtown and get ourselves a piece of real meat."

The trio stood up in unison and dumped and stacked their trays. The cook watched as they did it but never ventured a comment.

Above: The Japanese gillnetter *Jinmei Maru 8* carried a great deal of sophisticated fishing equipment as did the other three vessels seized in Alaskan waters for illegal salmon fishing. Below: Two of the four Japanese gillnetters can be seen nearing Coast Guard dock at Kodiak after their capture. (Photos courtesy Lt. Cmdr. Robert H. Stracener)

Waters in Woman's Bay were placid when the above photos were taken of the Japanese fishing fleet tied up at the U.S. Coast Guard dock. Both vessels in the lower photo are riding rather low in the water with their tons of salted salmon stowed below decks. (Photos courtesy Lt. Cmdr. Robert H. Stracener)

"Did you ever see such a mob of people before in your life?" Glass asked as they filed down the gangway.

Boatswain's mate third class "The Pub" Puderbaugh looked around at the dock briefly, then answered, "Hell, these people on the dock are all officials. You should see the mob at the gates of the base. They tell me the town's entire population is down here for the event."

"The Pub" was right, Glass thought, as they were forced to fight their way through the crowd at the gate. After considerable difficulty they managed to get beyond the crowd and catch a cab for Kodiak proper. Dismissing the cab as soon as they entered the downtown area they continued along the street in their quest for a restaurant.

"You know anything about this town?" Glass asked, not really directing his question to either of them in particular.

"It's my first time," volunteered "The Pub," "but if you are concerned about a cafe I understand there are several of them here. Looks like one right up there ahead."

They walked a little farther, then Glass turned to them again asking, "Say, what the hell was wrong with Moose? I saw you two helping him off the fishing boat back there awhile ago."

"Hey, now, that's a real story," Seaman Dennis said. "You know each one of those boats was carrying an extra supply of one thing or another—enough for the whole group. Well, the old *Maru No. 19* was carrying enough suntori for the whole fleet, and old Moose was bound and determined that he wasn't going to leave any of it untouched."

"Yeah," chimed in "The Pub," "the first damned day we are on the tub he gets himself smashed and decides to take a nap on the mess-hall table. When it came time for the Japanese to eat, it took six of them to move him into the berthing area so they would have a place to eat their chow. Then when it came time for beddy-bye, three of those Japanese had to sleep on deck because he had that much space tied up."

"We finally got him up at 3 a.m. for his watch, and you know what the big ape did? He headed right for the raw salmon and seaweed, washing it down with more suntori. He's been drunk the whole trip. We never did get much out of him except snoring."

"Wouldn't you know it," Glass said, "you guys get all the booze and I wind up on the boat with an abundance of Japanese cigarettes, which I hate with a passion."

They walked for a while before "The Pub" related, "You know that damned Moose can talk some alley Japanese, and he had those clowns giving him anything he wanted. I'll bet he saw his share of geishas, Datsuns and white elephants on that trip! Wouldn't surprise me if it didn't take him at least a month to sober up. Me, I had to pay for whatever I got."

"You sure as hell did," Dennis shot back. "Hell, he traded four rolls of s--- paper for three bottles of suntori, and he took the paper out of our survival box at that."

"Well, you can just be damned thankful I wasn't like Moose and didn't try to drink it all before the trip was over."

"I'll bet you would have if you thought that you could have gotten away with it," Dennis said. "You just happened to know that Ensign Conway was not about to let two of you get away with being drunk, and you happen to be the junior petty officer."

"All I can say is that you guys were pretty lucky," Glass said as they looked in the window of a likely cafe. "We not only didn't have any booze aboard, but there were just the two of us to stand all the watches."

"What happened to Dempsey and Franklin? I saw them go over with you the first day?" asked "The Pub."

As they settled down at the table in a far corner of the cafe, Glass started telling them the story of the seasickness and the bobbing boat. As the two looked at the menu they shook their heads in disbelief.

While Glass continued with the story the waitress interrupted with, "Are you fellows from the *Wachusett?*" Then as she pulled her pencil out of her hair to write down their order, "My husband is a Coastie stationed here."

The three looked up at her and nodded in the affirmative, and with that she went on to say, "Sure wish my husband could get transferred down to Seattle. I hate it here." She looked at them as though expecting some sympathy, then continued, "It seems like the sun just never shines, and the wind never stops blowing. I don't know how much longer I'm going to be able to stand it."

The trio just sat and listened to her ramble on for a few minutes, and then were forced to butt in with requests for the biggest steaks to be had. They all ordered a beer to drink while they were waiting for the meal. Even while she was writing the order the waitress went on and on with how both she and her husband hated everything about Kodiak.

"Now, there is a real talker," said "The Pub" as she walked away to place their order. "I wonder how her husband ever got her to shut up long enough for him to propose?"

"Propose what?" Glass asked.

"Anything you can think of," one of them answered.

"You have to bear in mind she never said anything about having children," Glass shot back.

"Good gosh, you weren't thinking about something like that, especially with a brother Coastie's wife," said Dennis—then started to laugh.

"What the hell," Glass retorted, "when I'm at home I do it with a Coastie's wife, don't I?" and with that the three of them fell silent nursing their beer, all too tired even to joke.

24. THE EVIDENCE

Lt. Stracener appeared rather nervous as he descended the gangway of the *Wachusett* the morning after arriving in Kodiak. He had been summoned to take part in the evaluation of facts involving the Japanese. It was a task that he wasn't looking forward to.

He could well recall the afternoon before when they had pulled in to tie up. He had tried for what seemed like hours to turn over the responsibility of the *Maru 8* to the National Marine Fisheries Service. Each office at base headquarters he visited that afternoon would merely refer him to another. Finally, in desperation, he was able to make his desires known to another Coast Guard officer and the officer had assured him there wasn't much he was going to get accomplished that afternoon. It was then that he assumed his duties in that regard were over, at least for the time being. However, he was forced to promise to be back the following morning before being released to return to the cutter.

The officer, who was attached to headquarters, had led him to believe they would want him to sign affidavits and produce the pictures he had taken while aboard the fishing boat. As he trudged on, it was his opinion that if things were not better organized this morning, there would be little doubt of its being a long, trying day.

On entering headquarters, he had very little difficulty finding one of the several rooms where information was to be assembled.

He was instructed to sit down, and after what seemed like days of waiting he was asked to present whatever it was he had in the way of evidence. Briefly he told what had transpired during the time he was on the *Maru 8*. He described the pictures he had taken, as well as his estimate of the number of fish on board. Immediately his camera was taken over with the assurance they wanted to develop the pictures. He was asked if he would be willing to sign an affidavit regarding the fact that fish were in the hold of the ship when he went aboard. He had expected that, so answered in the affirmative, and again he was asked to wait while the document could be prepared. It seemed like another lifetime before it was ready for his signature

While he waited, he could hear some of the other interrogation that was taking place in the room. He hadn't noticed it so much before but suddenly it became rather difficult even to keep his thoughts straight with all the noise in the place.

He didn't quite catch the name but it was now plain that a Coast Guard lieutenant, accompanied by a Fisheries Management agent, had spotted the offenders while on patrol in a C-130 aircraft south of Kodiak. According to the report, the time was logged at 1 p.m. Alaska Daylight Time. The patrol unit contacted a Japanese gillnet ship 55-58N, 142-40W. During the next hour and a half the patrol located three more Japanese salmon vessels, distributed along an east-west line for some 50 miles.

It was at this time that NMFS agent Zahn photographed each vessel, documenting the observations. As the aircraft circled each ship to be photographed, each ship cut its net and steamed south. Thus, each vessel abandoned an estimated one to three miles of net. As the chase moved out of the area, the C-130 dropped a radio marker beacon on the *Hokutatu 17* net at 1:40 p.m. A.S.T.

It was during this time that the lieutenant radioed Coast Guard headquarters in Juneau advising them of the situation, and headquarters diverted the cutters *Wachusett* and *Clover*, both some 100 miles north, to pursue and capture the Japanese. The CGC *Burton Island*, miles south, was directed north to intercept the chase.

The patrol plane flew repeated passes over each ship, dropping messages directing the vessels to stop. The messages were in both Japanese and English. Several messages, in English, were dropped telling the ships to go to Kodiak. A Coast

Guard helicopter from Kodiak, with NMFS agent Jim Branson, and U.S. Customs officer Al Knapp on board, flew to the scene at 4:45 p.m. and placed messages on each ship directing them to go to Kodiak. Customs Agent Knapp, fluent in Japanese, wrote the messages and confirmed the vessel names. Two of the ships turn for Kodiak briefly but soon resumed a southerly course out of the area.

Coast Guard C-130's and helicopters continued surveillance of the four ships that, still spaced in an east-west line, were traveling steadily south.

The Coast Guard cutter *Citrus,* commanded by Lt. Montonye, with NMFS agent William Dickenson aboard, departed Kodiak the same evening, July 12, and proceeded to the vicinity of some of the abandoned nets. Part of the fishing gear was located during the afternoon of July 13. The net was inspected, verifying the stretched mesh size of 4-1/2 inches, as well as the presence of salmon. The *Citrus* then remained on the scene.

It was on the 13th of July that the *Wachusett* and the *Burton Island* intercepted the Japanese ships and placed custody crews aboard. Later that day the cutter *Clover* assumed custody of two from the *Burton Island.* This move had allowed the *Burton Island* to resume her earlier mission. This was all news to Lt. Stracener, as he had been aboard the *Maru No. 8* during the time the chase and capture had taken place. When he returned to the *Wachusett* he had been too tired to discuss the incident at any length with other officers of the WA-WA.

It had been the *Wachusett* and the *Citrus* that escorted the four salmon boats into Kodiak on July 15. Of course, Lt. Stracener already knew that, but he was rather impressed by the amount of activity that had been going on both before and after the boarding crews had left the *Wachusett.*

He was feeling much better with himself and the entire situation when he left the base offices that afternoon. As he stood on the front steps of the office building, he knew that he would have to make a return when the evidence they would be presenting to the Japanese was completed, but right now things looked pretty good.

The weather hadn't improved a great deal, and he debated with himself whether to walk back to the cutter or take enough time off for an auto trip into Kodiak proper. It wasn't hard to convince himself that he would rather return to the ship and discuss events with fellow crew members in preference to being collared by some newspaper people outside the gate.

Lt. Stracener had been told not to discuss the matter with news personnel. Any news releases were to be made by the State Department, when and if they saw fit. That made the thought of mingling with civilians a little difficult inasmuch as the matter was still foremost in his mind and there were still a great many questions that he needed answers to. It had been the first time he had heard that the Japanese vessels had been steaming without lights throughout the chase. That information had been brought out by one of the aircraft pilots, and it was contrary to good navigation procedures, regardless of conditions.

It had also been news to Stracener that it was the *Maru 8* which had draped tarp over their identification figures on bow and stern when they realized that they had been sighted by a patrol plane. That sounded very much like something Fish Manager Yokoma would do, and the lieutenant could not doubt the authenticity of it because there were photographs to back the evidence. This would certainly blow a large hole, though, in Glass's theory. Glass had insisted that he didn't believe the crew members were aware of the fact that they had been fishing illegally, but if they had helped drape the tarp over the ship's identification, they would have to have an idea why they were doing it. Even after they had been aboard the *Maru 8*, he had noticed that the identification on the side of the fishing vessel's stack had masking tape over it. He had asked for an explanation of it then. Their answer had been that they had changed fishing companies, therefore did not fish for the same company the stack insignia depicted.

He hadn't thought too much about their explanation at the time, but now that he looked back on the matter, he recalled that they had changed the subject to the fact that they carried a red line around their hull and were permitted to have their cabin painted red. He hadn't followed the conversation all that close at the time. After all, it wasn't easy to determine some of their words as they translated into English. Yet it seemed, now that he tried to recall, that the red stripe and cabin were supposed to have some religious significance, and they were only allowed to use the red after they had completed three successful fishing trips during the season. They appeared to be rather proud of the fact they were eligible for it. There was a great deal more Stracener wanted to know about the event, and it was likely other officers could fill him in on some of the blank spots.

He didn't hurry on his way back to the ship, though; he even considered dropping by the *Maru No. 8*, just on the off chance that he could run into the crew member who had been a college student—and possibly learn a little more from him. As he drew nearer to the cutter he abandoned the idea and climbed the gangway.

Lt. Stracener headed directly for the wardroom, and was a little surprised to see that Ensign Mike Conway had completed his interrogation and had beaten him back to the ship. A little mental calculation told him that the ensign did not have the pictures of shipboard activities to explain, as he had, so that could account for it.

"Well, what did you think of the whole affair?" the ensign asked as he offered a cup of coffee to Lt. Stracener.

"You have to admit it was something different," the lieutenant commented as he accepted the cup. Even as he said it he was analyzing the ensign. They were both natives of Washington State, and in some respects alike. The ensign was a few years younger and a wee bit shorter, and was having difficulty holding his weight down. Yes, Lt. Stracener had to admit that he was glad he wasn't forced to jog up and down the decks of the *Wachusett* to fight off gaining additional pounds. Controlling the food intake had done the job so far for him, but not so in the case of the ensign.

"I suppose you have already heard that 'Moose' spent the entire trip about two-thirds drunk?" the younger man asked.

"No," Lt. Stracener answered. "How come you let him get away with that?"

"Well, I'll tell you," the ensign started to explain, "you know he has already received his replacement here, and most of the crew sympathize with the big guy. Oh, I know I could have sent him back to the cutter, but he did have a way of communicating with those Japanese, so he was of some value in that regard. I also knew that there wasn't any five of those fellows who were going to challenge anything that the rest of us did as long as he was around. Then for the clincher, I just couldn't see how we could successfully load him into the whaleboat at sea. It just looked to me as though a couple of us would wind up in the drink if we tried it. I guess that pretty well covers the situation. Now, what do you think you would have done under the same circumstances?"

Well, when you explain it that way, I just don't know," the lieutenant answered. "Thank goodness, I had some responsible assistance."

"How long do you think Glass would have stayed responsible if there had been plenty to drink around, like there was on our vessel?" the ensign asked, seriously.

"In that regard, I wouldn't worry too much. I think I know Glass about as well as anyone, and I'm reasonably sure that even if there had been plenty to drink aboard, he would have been around when I needed him. You can be sure of one thing, though, if I hadn't thought so I certainly would have asked for some relief when I sent Dempsey and Franklin back to the cutter. No, I'm convinced that it wouldn't have been much different even if there had been a lot to drink aboard—in spite of what Glass might tell the boys."

"I'll admit that you know him better than I do," the ensign replied, adding, "That is one thing you can say about this type of operation—you really can learn the inside workings of an individual when you spent so much time that close to them."

"How are the wandering boys?" interrupted Lt. jg Jones as he entered the wardroom.

"Fine," both men answered in unison.

"You fellows want some more coffee while I'm here?" Jones asked as he poured himself a cup and held the coffeepot up.

"Yes, I think I'll have some more," the ensign answered as he held his cup over in the lieutenant's direction for a refill.

"How about you?" Lt. Jones asked as he filled the ensign's cup, looking at Stracener as he said it.

"I suppose I might just as well as long as you have the pot over here," was the answer. When Jones had filled the cups he sat down across from the two, waiting for one of them to open the conversation.

"Say, do you know, has there been any disposition made on those fishing boats yet?" Stracener asked.

"Not positively," Jones answered, "it seems they are still trying to get a clear answer from the Japanese authorities. The National Marine Fisheries people are still considering sealing the holds and sending them back to Japan. Of course, they would have us fellows escort them out a ways, and then have some Japanese enforcement vessel pick them up for the balance of the trip. Nothing definite as yet though."

"Boy, wouldn't that be a lot of fun if we had to try and herd that bunch again?" Ensign Conway asked.

"You bet," Lt. Jones answered. "It wouldn't even be as easy as the last time around. I understand that the four captains are really on the Fish Manager's back about getting them so far inside the abstention line that they couldn't get back across without being caught. The captains are blaming him, and he is telling them that they are captains of their individual vessels so they didn't have to come if they didn't want to. Sounds to me like a real jolly get-together."

"I can see what you mean," Lt. Stracener said. "With them fighting among themselves, how in the world could we expect any cooperation out of them to stay in convoy formation?"

"Well, let's just hope that the Japanese government sends someone to pick them up," Ensign Conway commented.

"Still a little hard to believe that any of them would be dickering with the Fish Manager though," Lt. Stracener commented. "The crew on the *Maru No. 8* seemed to be deathly afraid of that man. He had them believing that he was something like the second coming."

"Well, maybe singly those captains were afraid of him, but get the four together and it is something else," Lt. Jones observed.

"You could be right," was Lt. Stracener's only reply.

25. SHORE LEAVE

There was just no describing how much better Glass felt the following morning after a full night's sleep in his own bunk. As he rolled out onto the deck, he recalled the times he woke up stiff and cold aboard the Japanese fishing boat, and thanked his lucky stars that the ordeal was over. That, coupled with a hot shower, another item he had sorely missed on the *Maru 8*, had him ready to challenge the world, as he headed for the mess hall and some hot breakfast.

Conversation in the mess hall seemed to be centered around the feelings in the Kodiak community relative to the Japanese fishermen. There were even comments of "Let's kill the bas-----!" being made by civilians ashore, according to at least one Coastie at the table.

Glass just sat there fingering his coffeecup as he continued to listen. For the life of him he couldn't feature why the people should be so worked up. Didn't they all know that the Japanese were not the only fishermen that were poaching in the Alaskan waters? Granted, the bulk of them hadn't invaded the waters as deeply as these four had, but what difference did it make whether they were robbed from the porch or from the living room? It was still stealing, whether it was taking candy from a baby or holding up a bank.

Finally, he couldn't contain himself any longer and piped up so most could hear him, "I don't know why everyone is so up-tight. Those fishermen were merely doing what they were told to do. I don't believe there were more than a handful on all four boats that knew that they were actually in illegal waters." Now that he had gained the attention of a great many of his fellow crewmen, he continued, "Sure the officers knew, but judging from what I saw and heard, those Japanese didn't have the vaguest idea where in hell they were fishing until we came aboard. And another thing—that damned Fish Manager of theirs would as soon have cut our throats as look at us—except that the crew was friendly and cooperative enough that he felt he didn't dare."

"You go out there and get yourself up on a soapbox and preach all of that crap you want to," someone shot back at him, "but when you get all done, those folks will still string you up right alongside those slant eyes. Those folks are mad and you better believe it! You have to remember these people all depend on fishing as a means of staying alive. Just about everyone here is either a fisherman or dependent on the industry. If I were you, I would take the same tack that Rodgers here is taking," and nodded in the direction of another Coastie sitting at the table. "He has those folks believing that he brought all four boats in single handed, and he's become a hero. As a matter of fact, he didn't have to buy a drink all night, and you better believe he really drank his share."

Glass glanced over at the second Coastie and had to admit to himself that the fellow had all the outward signs of having over-indulged the night before. Hell, he told himself, I suppose the guy is right. There isn't much point in me trying to defend the Japanese fishermen's action. I might better keep my feelings to myself, at least while I'm in Alaska.

In spite of all that was being said about the Japanese, Glass felt a little sorry for the fishermen. Thinking back, he had been one of those who had tricked them into bringing their nets to the surface, and he had been one of the group who had convinced them they should radio the others to surrender. Of course, as it turned out it wouldn't have been necessary because there were additional Coast Guard vessels in the area. Even though they might not have been able to elude the Coast Guard in the long run, he was sure that by their action they had brought the matter to an earlier conclusion than might have occurred otherwise.

As he continued to kick the situation around in his mind he headed for the galley. It was just a matter of a few steps from where he had been toying with his coffee cup. Just as he was dropping a few oranges into a sack he had picked up, one of the cooks asked, "What in the hell do you think you are doing?"

Glass just looked around at him and continued to drop oranges into the sack from a crate under one of the work tables. Then as the cook stood over him, he explained, "Well, you know I was out on that tub for a few days and I just have a craving for some oranges. Seeing as how I plan to go ashore for the day I thought I would take a few with me. You got any objections?"

"All I can say is that you must plan on doing a lot of exercising to work up enough appetite to eat all those oranges," the cook said.

"Who knows, maybe I won't want to eat alone," Glass commented as he twisted the top of the sack and headed out of the galley. The cook stood and looked at him, scratching his head, until Glass had rounded the corner and was lost from sight.

Glass ambled the few hundred feet from the *Wachusett* to the *Maru 8*. The dock seemed void of people as he strolled along. It was pretty evident that the Japanese had been restricted to their own vessels for the time being. Perhaps for their own safety. If they hadn't been, it seemed they would have been stretching their legs with a walk along the dock at least.

Glass was startled from his thoughts as two seagulls swooped extremely close to him. The pair would have perhaps gone unnoticed if they hadn't been screaming at each other. They appeared to be fighting over a small piece of fish, and were completely ignoring the Coastie strolling along what they considered their private domain.

He was still mentally cursing the gulls out for causing him to stop short as he jumped down to the deck of the *Maru 8*. The tide must be out, he told himself as he struck the fishing boat's deck a little harder than he really wanted to. The noise resounding through the vessel caused a couple of the fishermen to come to the door of one of the passageways. On seeing Glass they turned and passed the word to other crew members. In no time at all he had a group of them around him.

The fishermen reacted like children around a tree on Christmas morning as he passed an orange to each. It was obvious from their faces and chattering that they not only appreciated the gift, but also the fact that he had thought enough of them to return to their boat after being relieved the afternoon before.

Glass began to wonder if he had done the right thing when the Japanese took turns pumping his hand, bowing, and making him feel that he had turned the keys to Kodiak over to them. Even though he enjoyed seeing them happy, he wasn't much for this thank-you routine that they seemed to be overplaying. After all, the oranges were not a pardon for their illegal fishing.

Glass backed away from the enthusiastic fishermen as fast as he could, but found himself trapped when he couldn't jump back to the dock level. From where the deck of the fishing boat was with the tide out, it had been a pretty good-sized jump down and certainly more than he could jump up.

He gave a frightened look around for something he could use as a step, but in the end was required to use sign language to get the help of one of the fishermen for a boost. The whole group of men wanted to help him, with the result that he was almost thrown up to the dock, scrambling to maintain his balance while the men below waved, giggled and bowed to him in turn.

After gaining the sanctuary of the dock again, he made his thank-you for the boost rather short. He was in a hurry to get away before he himself might show some emotion over their display of gratitude. If there was anything he couldn't stand it was people getting all sentimental about a thing like that.

He had originally planned to go ashore alone, but now as he passed close by the *Wachusett* on his way to the gates of the Coast Guard base, he changed his mind and swung down the gangway to the cutter's deck. After exchanging salutes with the deck officer he headed for the mess hall, knowing that he would encounter someone there who would be willing to spend the day ashore with him.

The Japanese fishing boats were still the main topic of conversation as he entered the mess hall. Ambling over to the coffee maker in the corner of the hall, he picked up one of the mugs and filled it as he looked around, trying to figure out who he would enjoy spending the afternoon ashore with. Finally he made his choice and put his cup down next to where Petty Officer Mel James was sitting.

Glass had never been what you could call close to James during the two years they had been together on the cutter. The duties of the two were so alien to each other they seldom came in contact except at mealtime, and even then they usually picked other personnel to sit and chat with.

James was a quartermaster and spent a great deal of time on the bridge of the vessel, and when he wasn't on duty he was usually apart from the rest of the crew either reading or writing to his wife back in Seattle.

Glass opened the conversation with, "Say, James, how would you like to go ashore and hoist a few this afternoon?"

James turned, looking him straight in the face. It was apparent he was trying to figure out what, if anything, was on the other's mind. After a full minute of trying to read Glass's mind he answered, "Sounds like a good idea. I sure don't care much about hanging around here and listening to another rehash of this Japanese caper." With that, he tipped his cup up and drained whatever coffee was still there. He then looked down at Glass's full cup and commented, "Why don't you finish your coffee while I go forward and pick up some letters I want to get into the mail? I'll meet you right back here in a little bit," and with tht he swung his feet over the top of the bench and disappeared down the passageway.

Glass continued to sit and work on the coffee he had in front of him. As he waited he wondered why he had never made an effort to get better acquainted with James. They were both about five feet eleven and probably within five pounds of 160. They were pretty much alike in their general appearance, near the same age, both family men and seemed to have much in common. Just one of those things, Glass thought. In the liberties that he had been on, he rarely remembered running into James, and back at the base in Seattle, several of the crew members socialized while off duty.

At the moment, Glass couldn't recall any of the other crew members mentioning having been to James's home or vice versa. Still he knew that James was married and that he would take a few drinks on occasion. Maybe he could fathom the other guy better after this excursion, and if he wasn't his type he could always get "Buck" or Kelly to go along. Now that he thought about it, he wondered why he hadn't chased one or both of them down to start with. Anyway, the deed was done now and there was no point in sweating it.

Glass was still deep in thought when James showed up with a handful of envelopes saying, "Well, are you ready to go do it?"

"Oh, sure," Glass answered as he set his empty coffee cup on the counter and turned to get in step behind James.

26. THE SECRET

As soon as the two Coast Guardsmen drew within eyesight of the gate to the base, it was apparent the Japanese were still an item of importance. Although it was difficult from that distance for the pair to tell, people congregated at the gate did not appear to be what would be termed local citizens. As the two flashed their identification cards for the guard at the gate, it was obvious the crowd was made up mainly of press people. At least it seemed that way from the amount of cameras visible and the fact that some even had a suntan.

"I can't see why those newspaper people are clamoring around the gate," Glass said as they elbowed their way through. He looked at James, seriously hoping he had some type of answer.

"You got me," James replied, appearing just as concerned at that point as Glass had been. He added, "I would think the Coast Guard would be tickled to death to have this chance to take a bow. After all, it isn't every day that four illegal fishing boats are picked up," and with that the two continued on their way.

"There is one consolation," Glass commented. "I understand under ordinary circumstances a person has to call a cab from here and then wait a while until it gets here from town. There doesn't seem to be any waiting now. I've seen cabs galore hanging around the gates ever since I've been here," and with that he signaled one of three cabs waiting for a fare.

"'How far is it to town anyway?" James asked as they climbed into the back and told the driver they wanted to go to town. Before Glass could venture a guess, the cabbie answered, "It's right close to eight miles, give or take a few feet." Then he looked around at the two as though he might be in doubt as to their financial ability, and added, "The fare is $7.90 one way."

"Don't get worked up," Glass said, "I think we can empty our piggy banks and come up with enough money to pay the bill. Just get us there in one piece." The cabbie immediately turned back to his driving.

After they had alighted from the cab and were walking along the streets of the city, they paused in front of a likely looking bar.

"Let's stop in here and see what gives," Glass said after they had gone a few blocks with little or no conversation between them. As he said it he looked around at James for an answer. The only indication he received that James had even heard him was a nod in the affirmative, and so the two entered.

"You want to sit at the bar or table?" James asked as they stood inside the dimly lit bar letting their eyes get accustomed to the darkened interior. Even though it was another cloudy day in Kodiak, the subdued light inside made it hard to distinguish what was at hand.

"Aw, let's sit at the bar, then the bartender won't have to haul the drinks so far," and with that, Glass grabbed one of the nearby stools and motioned for James to take the one on his right.

Looking around the place now, Glass could see that there was a group of three men at the far end of the bar, drinking. They just had to be fishermen, he thought. All three appeared to have at least a two-day growth of beard and were wearing typical marine foul-weather gear. Down the bar, about halfway between them and the fishermen, another man sat alone. At a glance, Glass didn't want to venture a guess at what his occupation was. He certainly didn't look like the average fisherman, and he definitely wasn't a Coastie. He was probably a civilian employee on the Coast Guard base Glass thought, as he brought his attention back to James.

"What are you going to have?" James was asking. The bartender was standing in front of them now, waiting for Glass to make him up mind.

"Oh, I'll just have a bottle of beer," he muttered, at the same time realizing he hadn't heard James order.

"Okay, so you guys want a couple of beers. What flavor?" the bartender asked as he started back up the bar rattling off several brand names as he went.

"Hell, I don't care, just so it is cold," both Coasties said almost in unison.

"You fellows off the cutter?" the bartender inquired as he set the two bottles of beer down in front of them. He then explained that he knew about all the Coasties that were either stationed there or aboard the buoy tender *Citrus* which operated out of that port.

"Yeah," Glass answered, then turned to see if James was interested in commenting.

He noticed that James was looking over his shoulder on down the bar, and just as he was turning back around to see what it was that interested him so, a voice almost in his ear asked, "Mind if I join you?"

Before anyone could even answer, the man was taking a stool beside him. Glass said, "Suit yourself." Even as he said it he knew that he had wanted to get better acquainted with James, but that would evidently be out of the question, at least for the time being.

"I'm with the National Marine Fisheries Service," the stranger pointed out, as though it was supposed to have some special meaning for the two. Both just waited to see what he really had on his mind. After a pause he continued, "Well, you know how it is, we're not supposed to say anything about those Japanese fishing boats, but at the moment what else is there to talk about?"

Without even waiting for James to speak up, Glass asked, "What do you mean we aren't supposed to say anything about them? No one said anything to us about not talking," and as he said it he turned to James. "At least they haven't to me. How about you?"

James was quick to answer this time with, "Nothing's been said to me," then added, "Hell, they wouldn't figure we knew enough to talk about it anyway."

Glass nodded agreement, and they both looked back at the newcomer for further explanation.

"I don't know exactly where the orders came from, but I do know that somebody back in Washington, D.C., has passed the word to keep this as hush-hush as possible, and that is pretty difficult in a small town like Kodiak."

"How in the hell can they expect to keep something like this from getting out?" Glass asked and before anyone could answer added, "I'll just bet that's why all the newspaper guys are hanging around the gate."

"You better believe the newspaper people are hot on this one," the newcomer said, smiling. "You should see the news release that our office has put out to them. It merely tells the names of the Japanese vessels and where they were caught. Certainly would be hard for anyone to really make a story from it. Although, according to the news on radio, Governor William Egan isn't keeping the matter a secret. He's talking about turning the Alaskan fishermen loose to fish without any bag limits and all that junk. Of course, he couldn't get away with it, but he can sure shake a few timbers, which he's doing. I understand that Senator Ted Stevens plans to make a big issue of it back in the Capitol, but that remains to be seen. Most of those politicians are all talk and no action. Once in a while you'll run across one that's trying to earn his pay but they are few and far between."

In the course of a few beers and a lot of discussion, the National Fisheries representative related that their people were presently working with the Coast Guard officers involved, putting together all the evidence on the violation.

"How long you think they will have to hang around?" Glass asked, referring to the Japanese. He was curious because again that morning the fishermen had tried to get an indication from him as to how long they would be detained.

"Well, you know they won't be tried here," the NMF man said.

"What do you mean, they won't be tried here?" Glass asked, really surprised.

"I've got it right here," the other said as he pulled some papers out of his pocket and started reading: "When any. . . fishing vessel is actually engaged in operations in violation of the provisions of this convention. . .arrest or seize such vessel. . . and deliver such vessel. . .as promptly as practicable to the authorized officials of the Contracting Party to which such vessel. . .belongs at a place to be agreed upon by both parties." Then it goes on down here a little further and says: "Only the authorities of the Party to which the above-mentioned. . .fishing vessel belongs may try the offenses and impose the penalties therefore." With that he folded the paper up and placed it back in his pocket adding, "So you see we are just getting things ready for the Japanese when they come to get their friends and take 'em back to the homeland."

"When do you think that will be?" Glass asked, seriously interested now.

"All I can say is, there was supposed to be someone here from the Japanese Embassy, but as yet no one has showed, so no one around here seems to know how long they will be around."

"That's a hell of a note," James said, entering the conversation for the first time for several minutes. "I have the sneaking idea that we are going to have to hang around here as long as they do."

"That I wouldn't doubt for a minute," the NMFS man commented, then asked, "Say which one of our boys did you have with you?"

Glass didn't have the faintest idea what the fellow's name was. He had seen him around the cutter occasionally, but the guy had stuck to the bridge most of the time.

James had held back expecting Glass to answer; then seeing the puzzled look on his face he realized he didn't know. So he volunteered, "The guy's name was Hammond. You see, being a quartermaster I spend a great deal of my time on the bridge and that's why I happened to know him." The explanation was more for Glass's benefit than for the NMFS man.

"You knew he was formerly a Coastie, didn't you?"

"Yes, I gathered that from the conversation one day on the bridge. I believe he said he was a lieutenant and was in for two years. He must still be in his twenties," James replied.

"Glass here was on one of the boarding parties," James said, warming up to the discussion. "He has the idea that those Japs didn't realize they were in illegal water until they had been boarded. That is, with the exception of the officers."

The NMFS representative turned to Glass as though he couldn't believe what he heard, then said, "Don't ever kid yourself on that score." He waited a couple of minutes to see what Glass's reaction would be, then went on, "When those fishing boats were first spotted, one of them had tarp draped over their identification on the bow, bridge and stern, even had masking tape on the stack insignia. It was only after continual passes by one of the aircraft that they managed to get a picture when a breeze was blowing, and with that we were able to make a positive identification. You certainly can't convince me that the crew of that boat didn't know they were playing ball in someone else's park."

"Damn, that is hard to believe, from the way the crew acted on the tub I was on," Glass countered.

"Well, I'm not going to say that is true in all cases, but you sure have to admit they knew about it when one of our choppers took the Japanese interpreter out and told them over the loud speaker, in both Japanese and English, they were off base and must proceed into Kodiak. I don't know if the boat you were on was one of them that started toward Kodiak after the instructions, but whichever one it was swung around and made a run for it again as soon as the plane got out of sight. Actually there were two of them that tried that caper. Now those people all had to know it was a game of cops and robbers."

"I don't see why," Glass said, "but I still feel sorry for those poor clowns that were on our tub. What a life!"

"Say, fellows, I didn't realize how late it was getting. I'm going to have to get the heck out of here. I've got to get something to eat and then some shuteye. After all, I go back to the papers again early in the morning," and with that the NMFS man tipped his glass to empty it and started sliding off the stool.

"What time do you get off tomorrow?" Glass asked.

"I'll be off about 2:30 or 3:00 again like today. Why?" he countered.

"I thought maybe if you were going to be around again tomorrow, I could give you an answer as to whether those crew members knew they were illegal before the planes spotted them," Glass answered.

"Okay, I'll stop in when I get off," the other said, adding, "Maybe I'll have a little more low-down on the situation myself then." As he headed for the front door he turned and waved saying, "Good to chat with you guys, and see you tomorrow."

"What do you think?" Glass asked James. "You think we should get something to eat ashore, or head back and see what that cook fouled up for chow?"

"Oh, let's head back," was the answer. "I've got some writing to do and I'm posted for duty at midnight."

"Hell, you just mailed a handful of letters a little while ago," Glass said, and before James could say anything added, "How about tomorrow? You want to come over and talk with the guy again?"

"You bet I do," James was quick to reply. "I'll meet you in the mess hall about two tomorrow. That will give you a chance to go over and pump some information out of your Japanese friends." As he said it he gave Glass a broad smile and pat on the shoulder.

Glass ignored the last remark, not sure whether there wasn't a touch of sarcasm connected with the "Japanese friends" bit. He figured there was little point in making an issue of it. However, one thing was for sure and that was the certainty that he was going to check into the matter some more.

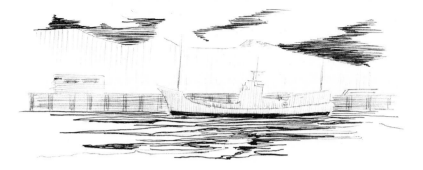

27. INTERROGATION

Things were still being operated on a standby basis aboard the *Wachusett* the following day. The bulk of the crew were allowed liberty privileges, with only a skeleton force drawing duty.

Glass was up early, and after a shower and a cup of coffee, he decided he had best follow James's example and get a letter off to the wife back in Seattle. He certainly had no way of telling how much longer they would be tied up in Kodiak. Under normal conditions they would have been on their way back to Seattle by now. Word had spread that the original scheduled trip into Anchorage was off, but that didn't mean they would head directly south either.

He didn't bother trying to find seclusion for his letter writing; he just moved his coffee to the end of one of the tables. There was a considerable amount of noise in the mess hall with crew members coming for breakfast and chattering about happenings of the previous day, and week. He was rather accustomed to it and had learned to cope with the confusion while still being able to concentrate on his writing.

Most of the crew members realized what a chore it could be trying to concentrate on writing letters home and had a tendency to soft-pedal their remarks around someone in the process of writing.

That morning Glass's desire to write seemed to be contagious because before long there were Coasties scattered throughout the mess hall either reading letters in preparation to answering, or in the act of writing.

Glass intended to write only one letter, and that was going to be to his wife; he had long since made it a practice to let her do the family corresponding. He had been a little concerned about his wife. She hadn't been sick, but she hadn't really been well, either, and now with her a few months into pregnancy he was sure that she would welcome a letter from him. He had slipped away during the time he and the other Coasties had been at the cafe and called her. But because of the time difference between Seattle and Kodiak he had got her out of bed. She had assured him that everything was fine there, and that had been his primary concern. They had talked only for a moment, not just because of the cost, but more because he didn't want the others to know of his concern for his wife. He had, however, assured her that he would write a letter as soon as possible.

He debated at some length as to whether he should mention the fact that he had spent a few days aboard a Japanese fishing boat as a member of a prize crew, and then decided against it. After all, there would be time enough for that when he got home; all she would do would be to worry about it. What she didn't know she couldn't worry about. He figured if she did happen to see something in the papers about the *Wachusett* being involved in the capture, she wouldn't think of him being a member of a boarding crew.

He didn't bother to spend a great deal of time on the letter. In the first place, by leaving the Japanese incident out, there wasn't much to put down. In the second place, he was eager to get to the *Maru 8* and see what he could find out. Under ordinary circumstances he couldn't have cared less about the disposition of the Japanese crew members, but he had a sort of empathy for several of these. After all, he thought, how could a person spend that much time with them without having some type of feeling for their future? He stuffed the two sheets he had written into an envelope and shoved it into his pocket, figuring to mail it later.

The cook didn't even bother to say anything to him as he tossed a few apples and oranges into a sack that morning. He just seemed to be so engrossed in whatever it was he was preparing that he completely ignored the move. Glass figured that he was busy with some concoction for lunch and didn't have time to harass anyone about a little fruit.

As he strutted down the dock toward the *Maru 8*, he wasn't nearly as preoccupied as he had been the previous morning. Now he knew what he wanted, and that was to get a few questions answered. He wasn't at all sure exactly how he was going to go about it just yet, but he was reasonably sure a little conversation with their one English speaking crew member should clear up a lot of things.

He hadn't much more than put a foot aboard the fishing vessel when the entire crew circled around him. He passed the fruit among them, and as he did he noticed that the captain had humbled himself enough to come forward for one of the gifts. Glass deliberately forced him to wait until all the rest had received theirs before he handed one over to him. The Fish Manager wasn't anywhere to be seen, but Glass was sure that he would not have given him one anyway. If there was anyone in the crew that he thought should get what he deserved in the way of penalty, that was the fellow.

After the crew were deeply occupied in devouring the choice morsels, Glass drew Charlie aside, together with the English-speaking crew member. He lost no time getting into the interrogation he had planned.

Foremost in his mind was whether or not the crew members were aware of the fact that they were fishing illegal waters prior to the patrol planes buzzing them. Of course, there was little doubt they would have known about it when the helicopter swooped in with the interpreter—if, in fact, this was one of the fishing boats they had done it with.

The information wasn't easily forthcoming. It took a great deal of asking and re-asking before it was finally brought out that Charlie had been reasonably sure they were illegal, but as far as the crew members were concerned, there would be no way of their having the knowledge; that is, unless they had overheard the Fish Manager or captain speak of it, and that seemed very unlikely. However, through the interpreter Charlie admitted a couple of crew members should have become suspicious when they had tried to conceal their identity by dropping a tarp over the stern and bow of the boat.

That made Glass feel a little better, to think that he hadn't been completely wrong when he said he doubted that the crew knew they were fishing illegally.

He was quite surprised to see the excitement they displayed when he conveyed the news that they would be taken back to Japan to stand trial. He thought they would be delighted with the news, but the result seemed to be the exact opposite. It appeared that Glass had given them the worst possible message. He was never able to get an understandable answer as to why they should be so shaken up about it. Judging from the reaction to the news, he decided he had gained about as much information as he was going to. As he started to leave, several of them went into their act of bowing and smiling, similar to their action when he had first boarded the boat. This gave him the feeling they were going formal on him again and he didn't like it at all.

With a tip of his hat he headed back toward the cutter, feeling he had lost ground with them.

It was a dejected Glass that strolled into the mess hall. It wasn't quite two o'clock but James was sitting there toying with a cup of coffee. He didn't make a move, just waited for Glass to grab some coffee and join him.

"You ready to go?" Glass asked as he let his frame slide down into a seat.

"I sure can't drink any more of this stuff," was James's only answer.

There wasn't any conversation between the two as they left the cutter, each waiting for the other to open up. It wasn't until they passed through the gates that they both commented on the fact that there wasn't a single news person standing around. This was in definite contrast to what it had been the day before.

After making the cab trip into town and sharing the cost, they walked slowly down the two blocks to the bar where they had been the day before. Instead of sitting at the bar as they had previously, they chose a table. There were several more people in the place than there had been on their previous visit, so considered a table would be a better place to talk.

They hadn't been there very long when the N.M.F.S. man stepped through the door. He stood just inside, surveying the people sitting along the length of the bar, then turned and spotted them. He walked over to the table, obviously still not accustomed to the subdued light in the place. Plunking himself down in one of the empty chairs, he remarked, "Boy, I'll tell you I'm ready for a drink. It has been a pretty hectic morning around our office."

The N.M.F.S. man had barely sat down when Glass started with, "Well, I checked those boys out this morning. After a lot of questioning I found that the only people who knew for sure they were fishing illegally were the Fish Manager, the captain and the radio operator. Of course, I have to admit that they found out the minute the first boat spotted one of those patrol planes—the word spread so fast. I guess they really jumped on the radio and passed the word to the other boats."

"Of course, it goes without saying that the word must have passed fast when they realized they had been spotted. I really do think they believed they could get away with it though." The N.M.F.S. man explained that the group in his office were still trying to assimilate all the evidence to have it ready when a Japanese representative showed on the scene. "Say," he continued, tipping his glass slightly and eyeing the contents, "I found out today that they are expecting a Hirai, and he is supposed to be the Japanese Chief Fish Inspector. According to the report I saw, he is coming in on the *Konan Maru*. They tell me that is a Japanese whaling vessel. I can tell you right now that folks around here are not going to like the looks of a Japanese whaling vessel in port, and I can't say as I blame them. Anyway, that is one of the reasons we are in such a hurry to have everything ready for them. We don't want to give them any call to hang around."

"In that message about the Chief Inspector, did it happen to say when they would be arriving here?" James asked.

"No, that is the one thing that I couldn't find out, and I guess that is the reason the big boys are in a hurry to get all the evidence put together. They just don't want that whaling vessel around here, like I said before."

"Did you notice there are sure none of those news people around the base gates any longer? Suppose they have gotten tired of trying and have given up?" Glass asked.

"I'm sure, after the treatment they received here in the last couple of days, they figured that any information being released would be from Washington, D.C. It's a cinch we aren't putting anything out now at all, and I don't think your people are either. As near as I can find out, it is our State Department that told everyone to cool it. I guess they are afraid it might damage Japanese-American relations, or some other garbage like that," the NMFS man explained.

"Well, it was fun while it lasted," James commented.

"What the hell do you mean, it was fun while it lasted? You weren't out there bobbing around like a cork, trying to live on "C" rations, and wondering when those Japanese might jump you," Glass shot back.

"I forgot about that, especially since you smell so much better now," James replied with a smile, "but at least it's over now."

"There's one thing for sure, your fly boys got a real workout during the whole mess," the NMFS man ventured. It seems they had to keep a constant eye on those fellows starting with when they were first spotted. I understand they had their problems a few times when it was real foggy."

"We can both vouch for the foggy bit," James chimed in.

The NMFS man didn't even let the interruption bother his chain of thought, continuing with, "Seems a couple of those babies are wooden, and have so little metal on them they were hard to keep pinpointed. That, plus the fact that they were playing as many games as they could with the fog banks in the area."

"You know the thing that bothered me the most?" Glass asked. "It was those clowns throwing away so much of their catch."

"What do you mean?" the NMFS man seemed really concerned.

"Well, after we got them to pull their nets, they threw away about a third of the catch. Seems that if the fish had any marks on their head or gills they would just pitch 'em overboard. It looked as though they were only interested in keeping the prime fish, those with no marks on them," Glass answered.

"Hell, we don't have any of that information in our reports," the NMFS man stated. "All we are putting together is what they have in the holds now, and where we spotted them. However, I guess with that information alone they should be able to hang a good fine on them."

"You really believe that the Japanese government will penalize the fish companies?" Glass asked. "After all, they shouldn't lay it on the crew members. They didn't know what the score was."

"To be truthful with you, we have only heard about the penalties on a few occasions. In some cases they rap the offenders pretty good, and then there are a lot of cases where they only wind up suspending whatever sentence they put on. I guess it all depends on who you are and how much influence you have," the NMFS man replied.

Glass just sat there for a few minutes digesting what he had heard, then commented that he didn't see any reason why he should lose sleep over the situation. He figured his part in the play was over.

"Well, what do you think the Coast Guard and National Marine Fisheries Service will do if they move the fishing limit out to 200 miles?" James asked, and then before anyone could answer he added, "I imagine it will take a great deal more money to police the area."

"Oh, I'm sure it will take more money, but by the same token, you have to remember that the line will hold true for every country then," the NMFS representative answered. "Instead of being forced to determine if they are Russian, Korean, Chinese, Japanese, Polish or whatever, we will only have to know that they aren't United States before we go after them."

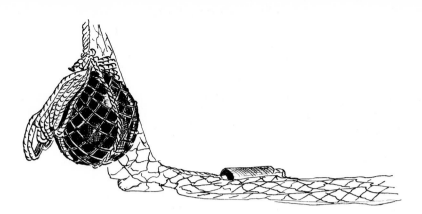

28. THE WHALER LANDS

Fishing boats and other marine activity are rather common around Woman's Bay; therefore when the *Konan Maru* materialized out of the mist, it went completely unnoticed by crew members of the *Wachusett*.

Even though the task of taking stores aboard had started and there were several crew members on deck, the arrival of the Japanese whaling vessel would have remained a secret to the Coasties had it not been for the big entourage of National Marines Fisheries Service and Coast Guard officials parading along the dock. The group appeared to be converging to welcome Japan's Chief Fish Inspector Harai, arriving aboard the vessel.

Only slightly larger than the other Japanese fishing boats being detained in harbor, the whaler carried a boom and winch on her forward deck, but she also carried the same international orange color. Though she had pulled up and moored close to the other Japanese, there appeared to be little recognition passing between her crew and the crew of the new arrivals. The entire affair gave the impression that it was perfectly all right to fish in illegal waters—but they were very remiss in having been caught in the act.

It would have been hard to ignore the fact that a dignitary had put in an appearance, as the U.S. and Japanese officials paraded past the *Wachusett* on their way to the base offices with bulging brief cases.

"I don't see anyone bowing in that crowd," Glass said to another crew member as the group passed the cutter.

"Whatya mean bowing?" the fellow asked, looking puzzled by Glass's remark.

"Well, when we first went aboard the fishing boat, those Japanese fishermen spent most of the first and second day bowing

to the lieutenant and me," Glass replied, realizing that the rest of
the *Wachusett* crew didn't know what had taken place aboard
the fishing boats regarding the boarding crews.

Activity aboard the *Wachusett* had picked up considerably
during the mid-morning of July 19, as they started taking stores
on in preparation for departure. While the word had not become
official at that point, scuttlebutt had it they would be leaving the
next day. Because of their extended stay in Kodiak, the
Anchorage liberty had been scrapped in favor of a couple days
stop in Juneau on their return trip to Seattle. But before Juneau
they were going to have several more days of patrol work to do. It
seemed rather foolhardy to them because the word of the capture
of the four Japanese boats would surely have spread throughout
the fishing fleets of any nations near those waters. As a result, it
did not seem likely that any illegal craft would be likely to invade
U.S. waters for at least a few weeks. The crew, therefore,
thought that any patroling now would be an anticlimax to what
had been.

When word passed through the cutter that the whaling vessel
had arrived and was presently moored farther down the dock,
Coasties aboard the *Wachusett* showed their pleasure.

Certainly there would be no need for their presence in Kodiak
when the Japanese pulled out, and the sooner they left the sooner
the *Wachusett* could do likewise.

Taking on stores continued throughout the day with the finish-
ing touches completed the next morning. By noon they were
ready even though meetings between the Japanese and U.S.
officials appeared to be continuing.

It wasn't until after lunch that a small group accompanied the
short, stocky fish inspector to the dockside of the whaling vessel.
Farewells hadn't much more than been said when the first of the
five Japanese vessels started disconnecting their ties with each
other and the dock. There was no fanfare as they filed out of the
harbor one at a time, supposedly heading for the Orient. Their
estimated time of arrival in Kushiro, Japan, was given then as
August 2, 1972.

The Japanese hadn't much more than disappeared into the
mist on their journey east when the *Wachusett* dropped her
mooring lines and followed them out of the bay. They, of course,
were on a much more southerly course than those who preceded
them. It wasn't until November 2, 1972, that the U.S. Embassy in
Tokyo was informed that each of the four vessels had been ad-
ministratively penalized by being required to remain in port for

100 days, commencing April 30, 1973, thus missing the 1973 salmon fishery.

As members of the *Wachusett* made their round of liberty haunts in Alaska's capital city, there was little or no mention of their encounter with the Japanese fleet. The event had been all but forgotten by everyone except the local fishermen, who would be a long time forgetting. It would not only be the event that would dwell long on their minds, but also the other estimated 1,200 Japanese and Russian ships annually taking more than four billion pounds of fish from the North Pacific waters—action that could very likely damage the fishing grounds far beyond repair. The future for Alaska's fishermen seemed dim at best.

29. END OF A FINE SHIP

"Wow!" shouted Seaman Kelly as he made fast the bowline at Pier 90 in Seattle, the *Wachusett's* regular mooring spot when she was in her home port, "am I glad that trip is over."

"You act like you didn't enjoy it," Glass said with a sardonic smile from the rail where he had been standing during the docking.

"Naw, that isn't it at all," Kelly said. "I'm just glad that we are back. Now I can see my girl and tell her all about it."

"I guess you're right. I can't say that I'm not glad to be back too. Now I can check on how my last batch of beer turned out," Glass replied.

"Don't go drinking it all in one sitting," Buckingham said, as he moved up beside Glass. "Just remember you promised me some."

"You mean you still want more beer after getting as sick on it as you did back in Juneau?" said Glass as he turned to look at Buck.

"That was a whale of a good liberty we had, but you know that trip down from there, with the weather progressively getting warmer, did wonders for me. Anytime I get in Puget Sound I'm like a new man. So bring on your beer and I'll drink with the rest of them," Buck said, taking a deep breath and extending his arms as though he were going to hug the entire City of Seattle. Then in a different vein he looked at Glass and said, "You know, I half expected to see Boatswain's Mate Hughes here to greet us."

"Why would he be here?" Glass asked as he turned to look Buck square in the face.

"Well, you knew about the finger wrestling incident in Kodiak, didn't you?"

"Yea, I understand that he and Boatswain's Mate Barnes got into a little match," Glass answered, "and I understand that they had only been going for about five seconds and Hughes got his finger broken."

"Yes, but after that his finger was listing about 30 degrees to one side. Hughes piped up and told Barnes that since he had broken it he should be the guy to fix it. So Barnes gave it a good pull straight out and increased its length by about two or three inches," Buck said, adding, "Well, anyway, the next day that finger was swollen to the size of about three normal fingers. After sending him to the doctor, they shipped him off to Elmendorf Air Force Base up there. Then, after they worked on it, they flew him down here, so he has been here for several days. I wouldn't have been surprised to see him at the dock just dying to get his hands on Barnes."

"Well, maybe getting that finger fixed sobered him up enough that he doesn't wany any part of Barnes," Glass commented.

"You're probably right. But I'm still glad that I'm not in Barnes's shoes," Buck said.

As the crew paraded off the *Wachusett* that day, little did they realize that that cruise was the last that many of them would be making on the WA-WA. As a matter of fact, it was one of the last cruises the ship made. Those who were not re-assigned to other ships or stations stayed aboard for one more extended cruise, because in July of the following year she was de-commissioned. She had been commissioned in 1946, nearly 30 years before, had seen service on a variety of details, and had sailed to many parts of the world, including the Orient.

Even though Coast Guard officials were seeking an additional 14 million dollars to be added to their annual budget for the purchase of at least six new ships and 40 new jet patrol planes, the *Wachusett* was considered too old and expensive to maintain any longer. Leaving behind it approximately 38,000 Coast Guard personnel, some 7,000 civilians, 300 ships, and about 180 aircraft, the WA-WA was retired from the active list, to plow Pacific waters no more, for the Coast Guard or any other purpose.

The *Wachusett* displayed an image that in no way detracted from the tradition of the nation's oldest seagoing service, as her superstructure shined in the bright warm sun in July, 1973. She lay quietly at her mooring lines as her commissioning flag was lowered. Even as the ceremony took place, there were few aboard who had made the eventful Alaska cruise. After the commissioning flag had been folded, it was turned over to Lt. Commander Pearson, who had assumed command after the Alaskan incident.

Commander Forsterer was assigned as "Captain of the Port" in Portland, Oregon, shortly after the trip, and retired from the Coast Guard, May 1, 1975. Fred Glass was transferred to the Coast Guard's "Readiness" headquarters in San Francisco, California; while Lt. Stracener was re-assigned to the Electronics Engineering office at the Coast Guard headquarters, Washington, D.C. Lt. Commander Pearson also received re-assignment to C.G. headquarters, Washington, D.C. Other Coast Guardsmen aboard during the cruise have either left the service with the completion of their enlistment or have taken duties elsewhere around the world.

When the de-commissioning festivities were completed, and everyone had moved from her cabins and deck, the *Wachusett* was towed to Sand Point, in northwestern Washington. There was little doubt that she could have made the trip under her own power, but she was sadly void of the many Coasties she had served with and for, during the years she carried the commissioning flag proudly above her decks.

After several months of being totally ignored at the Sand Point dock, the *Wachusett* was again moved, this time down the Sound to Tacoma, Washington. Although there had been rumors she would be used for target practice, she was forced to bow to the wrecking torch. Wrecking crews went aboard in early 1975 and started the task of reducing to scrap a proud U.S. Coast Guard cutter. Even though none of her crews were on hand during the scrapping, there is little doubt they all hope her steel will be used to construct another ship as good.

EPILOGUE

"You may deceive all the people part of the time, and part of the people all the time, but not all the people all the time," Nevin May said, quoting a famous remark during a fisherman's meeting in Ketchikan. "I feel that a good many of us will have to put ourselves into the category of having been fooled for some time."

He was making the point that organization was needed not only to combat the foreign fishing fleets in the North Pacific but also to exert considerably more pressure on senators and representatives, if there were to be any hope for the future of the fishing industry. "As individuals, we might just as well throw in the sponge now," he said and continued, "While it is encouraging, the extension of foreign fishing limits 200 miles off our coast will not be the whole answer, but it will certainly be an improvement of present conditions."

"Even as May was making his point to fishermen in the Ketchikan area, the National Marine Fisheries Service and the Coast Guard were amassing evidence which they felt was to be for a Japanese trial, relative to the four gillnetters. Putting the facts down was nothing new for the men at Kodiak. They had done it several times in the past and felt sure they would be called on to do the same in the future. They were well aware of the feelings of the fishermen in the Kodiak area, but were not aware that fishermen throughout Alaska were meeting to promote some kind of positive action for the future.

Nevin May sympathized with the Ketchikan fishermen's feelings because they mirrored what he himself felt. He had been one of them for many years. Born in Oregon, he took to the fishing grounds early in life; first with his father on the Umpqua, Coos and Rogue rivers and later on a commercial boat out of Winchester Bay, even while serving a printing apprenticeship at the *Sutherlin Sun*, in southern Oregon. Fishing became his first love and he moved to Alaska shortly after serving in the military, fishing with various commercial fishermen in the area of Ketchikan before leasing, then purchasing, his first vessel from savings.

Now married, with a son, he continued his efforts to bring some type of justice to the Alaska fishermen. It was shortly after the aforementioned meeting in Ketchikan that the Ketchikan, Alaska Trollers' Association was formed, with May as the first president. The group later affiliated with other organizations in the Northwest to provide a louder voice in their behalf.

Alaska's Senator Ted Stevens, speaking of the Japanese incident, referred to it as the "most flagrant violation to date" by the Japanese, "and cutting loose those nets was even more reprehensible." At the time he said he was going to demand reparations to the Kodiak fishermen for the depletion of the salmon run caused by "the illegal high seas salmon fishery of the Japanese fleet off the coast." About the same time Alaska's Governor William A. Egan was demanding that the Japanese government levy stiff penalties against the four gillnetters.

News coverage of the incident was not only played down throughout the rest of the 49 states, but coverage in Alaskan papers was held to a minimum. Actually the series of events leading to the capture, and the holding of the Japanese vessels, should have merited front pages throughout the world, and could have led to the alerting of a great many uninformed citizens.

Don Holm, of the Portland *Oregonian* staff, writing from Kodiak at the time, stated in part: "The temper of the people in Kodiak is that of intense resentment, not only against the Japanese fishing fleets, but against our own State Department for what they believe is the ruthless use of the Alaskan fishery resources in the game of international politics. Although the news lid was raised somewhat after the indignant outbursts from Senator Stevens, Govenor Egan, and others, it has been clamped down again on the Coast Guard and the National Marine Fisheries, both of whom have been instructed not to release any more information about the high seas salmon poaching episode without specific clearance." (*Oregonian*, July 25, 1972)

Even though fishing groups throughout the United States, such as Northwest Steelheaders Association, the Isaac Walton League, and the Sierra Club, allowed the incident to pass with little or no comment in their meetings, fishermen in the 49th state were meeting on street corners, bars, cafes, wherever, to discuss the matter. It was another example, that pointed out they would have to do something about the upward trend of foreign fishing vessels invading U.S. waters. They realized that some type of action would be needed because the foreign vessels were already cutting too deeply into what remained of the resource.

Later that month, Alaska's U.S. Congressman Nick Begich told editors of the Kodiak *Mirror:* "If the Japanese salmon gillnetters—detained in Kodiak last week for fishing some 700 miles outside a line agreed upon by international treaty—aren't given severe penalties by the Japanese government. . .Japan's 'most favored status' should be changed. The most offensive thing I can imagine was the fact they cut 12 miles of plastic net and ran. . .that's an insult to our government. If the Japanese continue to pursue a policy of encroachment, we should re-examine the Japanese position on the taking of whales. I would rather play it on a cooperative basis."

The Mirror also noted: "In communications to both Secretary of State Rogers and Secretary of Transportation Volpe, Begich has also outlined the need for more stringent law enforcement. . .for more high-endurance Coast Guard Cutters. The Coast Guard out of Kodiak, he said, patrols 53.7 per cent of the coastline of America and for that large area has the smallest enforcement contingency of any nation."

Congressman Begich, Governor Egan and Senator Stevens made their stiff comments about the incident, but even then only if they were pressed for such statements by the Alaska newspapers that showed an interest.

An editorial in the April 1972 issue of the *National Fisherman* stated in part that the average yearly catch of Pacific salmon was more than 405 metric tons during 1964-1970, mostly spawned in the streams of Russia, Canada and the United States. The *National Fisherman* also stated that "Japan's contribution to the fishery is minuscule compared to that of the other three nations. The concern for rational conservation practices exhibited by Denmark and Korea in refraining from, or in phasing out, their high-seas net fisheries for salmon leaves only one nation in the world currently committed to that wasteful and destructive method of fishing: Japan."

Naturally, being right on the scene, the *Mirror* commented on the event editorially. In part they stated: "The agreement is at best a terribly lopsided thing. For one thing there isn't even one American fishing boat, let alone fleet, taking any of the fishery resources from anywhere within three thousands miles of the islands of Japan. The likelihood that any American would ever be found stealing fish from the Japanese is in the realm of the absurd. Yet the Japanese, together with the Russians and the Koreans (and soon the Chinese and others) have for many years been taking our fishery resources off our Alaskan continental shelf. And this piracy of our resources has been taking place without any form of payment to the people of Kodiak or other Alaskan fishing communities who now find their resources being depleted through fishing methods and policies which completely disregard any thought of conservation of the resources.

"It is time for more direct action. If the federal authorities are too timid to act, and act forcibly with armed might if necessary, then the people of Kodiak and of all Alaska, should demand that their state government assume this obligation and act to preserve our heritage, our resources, our way of life. . ."

Fishermen in Alaska, as well as those fishing the waters off Washington, Oregon and California agree that the extension of U.S. territorial waters from the present 3 to 12 miles will not save the U.S. fishing industry, but it would certainly be a step in the right direction. They can, and do, cite case after case where fishermen have been forced to leave the trade, if not for lack of fish, for regulations that have been imposed to save the future of a species.

Nevin May says that the formation of fishermen's organizations in Alaska has done a great deal to muster the support of the 49th state's legislators, but more support is needed if there is to be a solution. More legislators from states other than coastal states will be needed, and convincing them of the need is the major hangup, he explains.

In speaking on the subject to varying groups who might show interest, May points out that according to International North Pacific Fisheries Commission reports, both sockeye and coho catches have greatly increased among Japanese land-based fishing vessels.

Reports also point out, according to May, that all available evidence indicates that the sockeye available to Japanese high-seas fisheries are almost entirely of Soviet or Western Alaskan origin. Another disturbing thing about the reports is that the average weight of sockeye taken by the land-based driftnet fishery gives additional cause for concern. The average size of sockeye in this fishery has always been comparatively small—in recent years about 1.5 kg, which is about 3/4 the average size of sockeye taken by the mothership fishery and certainly much smaller than the average size of maturing sockeye returning to Western Alaska or the U.S.S.R. This strongly suggests that the land-based driftnet Japanese fishery takes a high proportion of immature sockeye year after year.

On more than one occasion May refers to a Summary of a Draft for the National Fisheries Plan, produced by the U.S. Department of Commerce. In the draft it is pointed out: "More and more fish are being taken off the U.S. Coast—but not by Americans. The harvest has increased from 4.4 billion pounds (round weight) in 1948 to 11.1 billion pounds in 1972. That's an increase of 6.7 billion pounds. Almost all of that increase has gone to foreign fleets. Why aren't Americans catching those fish?

"Americans are eating more and more fish—but much of it is imported. U.S. fish consumption went up from 3.9 billion pounds (round weight) in 1948 to 7.0 billion pounds in 1972, an increase of 3.1 billion pounds. Most of that 3.1 billion pounds has been caught by foreign fleets. Why not American fleets?

"We need to increase U.S. Fisheries production. The total production of the U.S. fishing industry has not increased over the years, even though some parts of it have—tuna, shrimp and crab. Why haven't other parts of the fishing industry done as well?

"We need to provide more seafood for increased U.S. consumption. Americans are expected to eat 3 billion pounds more fish in 1985 than they do today. Where will it come from?"

Regardless of how many figures are presented or what the figures point out, May contends that "moving the fishing limits out from the American coast and full control of foriegn fishing fleets will never come until enough people realize what it can mean to them as time goes on."

Emery Huntoon

The Author

Perhaps because of his three years as a U.S. Navy Salvage diver during W.W. 2, or possibly because he was recalled in the Korean conflict and served with the Navy for three more years, but certainly because he feels a closeness to the sea, the ships, and the sailors who man them, Emery Huntoon felt compelled to write about them.

He was barely out of school when he left Michigan to enter the Navy. This was the beginning of a life far removed from that of his boyhood. As a newspaperman in civilian life he worked from newsboy to composing room to editor-publisher of his own papers. He picked up several national and state awards for news writing, along the way and between wars, migrated to Arizona, then California and on to Oregon, where he now makes his home and loves it.

He had been hearing about the growing scarcity of fish and the infringement of the fishing fleets from other countries before his trip to Alaska in 1972, but the problem hadn't been his concern. He heard complaints from sport and commercial fishing friends of the lack of catches. Everyone had a reason for their complaints—but seldom was the reason completely valid.

When Mr. Huntoon's son-in-law, who was a Coast Guardsman just in from a cruise, started relating to him events surrounding the seizure of four Japanese fishing boats, he felt the story should be told. After a considerable amount of research and writing-counseling and much work, the result was— *Intercept and Board.*

Mr. Huntoon is presently the editor of the Oregon Teamster newspaper, vice-president of the Western Labor Press Association, president of Oregon Labor Editors and active in several civic and fraternal organizations. Between his wife, Margery, and himself they share 11 children, step-children and in-law children, along with 11 grandchildren. When time permits he enjoys golf, photography, traveling and needless to say, fishing.